WHEN MEN LEAN IN
We All Win

REVITALIZATION, EDUCATION, & REPRESENTATION

D1360340

WHEN MEN LEAN IN
WE ALL WIN

DR. LARRY WHITE SR.

TABLE OF CONTENTS

INTRODUCTION

Gerald A. Moore, Sr.

The black man is the foundation of the black family. But in America, the black man has been subjugated by the dominant power structure. Thus The wealth of the black family is predicted to be zero by 2050. What does this mean one might ask? It means that after 400 years of slavery, brutality, Jim Crow, segregation, oppression, the infusion of crack cocaine into black communities, the 1994 Crime Control and Law Enforcement Act signed by President Bill Clinton which launched the mass incarceration of black men to further destroy the black family by ensuring that the black man was removed and absent from the home and community. The school to prison pipeline upon which our government is complicit building prisons based on the reading levels of black boys by 4th grade. Which brings us back the question, what does this mean?

It means that at the rate we are going now my grandchildren and your children and grandchildren will be forced into indentured servitude setting the black family back 200 years. But "we've come too far to turn back now"; all of the bloodshed from our ancestor's, freedom fighters and those who lost their lives for the civil liberties that we have today. As a black man in this country, I am not willing to let the work of our heroes Nat Turner, Frederick Douglas, Marcus Garvey, Martin Luther King, Malcolm X, and the numerous black men who risk their lives during the civil rights movement go in vain.

Today in America the black man is in a state of emergency. We are at war with one another in our major cities across the country. Senseless violent crime and murder destroying husbands, brothers, uncles, and sons. How have we allowed outside forces to steal our humanity and turned us against each other and against a fervor for life.

But where one does not see hope I see opportunity. I am excited that at the writing of this book we are seeing a resurgence of the collective, black men who are ready to step up in unity and reclaim our position as kings. Ready to fight to restore the black family. Ready to fight for our black boys to allow them to survive. Ready to pour knowledge, wisdom, and understanding into the young black males in our communities who are lost because they have been taught to hate themselves therefore they have no compassion for the life of their brother.

I'm here to tell you today with renewed hope and faith in God our secret weapon that will heal all will be revealed by the black men whose stories you will witness in this book. The ultimate shield, the highest vibration, the most powerful force in the universe -- LOVE. We have tried everything else, but LOVE. LOVE will lift us above negativity, drama, and chaos. LOVE will bring us the strength and courage to do what's required to restore the black family and the black community.

As the title of this book suggests "When Men Lean In, We All Win". This concept has been foreign as we have been complicit in our demise. We have allowed our women to be forced to head of household. We disrespect, abuse, and allow others to mistreat our mothers, wives, sisters, and daughters to the point where they are beginning to lower themselves to believe that calling each other bitches and whores are worthy titles of empowerment.

But the men who will place their hearts on the pages that proceed will present a combined force of reclamation, a new beginning, a new opportunity for our humanity. This is the start of a revolution, where we show black men and boys how to LOVE. The black community needs leadership, a code of conduct presented as a unified front. Therefore, "When Men Lean In, We All Win" will be a matter of fact.

I am blessed to be a part of this project for I am a story of reclamation and redemption. I was very much on the path of self-destruction. I was a destroyer of my own community. At 15 years of age, I was in the "Scared Straight" prison deterrent program for at-risk teens. As a natural leader, I had a choice where I could lead those who followed down a path of criminal activity and mischief or down a path of righteousness and productivity. I'm fortunate that my God allowed me to see my divine gift as a leader of men. I have a clear understanding that I am a builder, not a destroyer and I'm obligated to create a pathway for those young black males and boys within my purview of influence.

"Let us not become weary in doing good, for at the proper time we will reap a harvest if we do not give up" (Galatians 6:9 , KJV).

This scripture is at the heart of a movement and will become the mantra of truth for "When Men Lean In We All Win". "Let us not become weary", powerful for as men we need to know when to pass the torch. I have three sons whom I'm grooming to take over on my behalf. They will groom their sons to proceed with them. Therefore we do not become weary, as our sons become men, the seeds sown will germinate across the black family and community producing a transformation of epic proportion in the harvest we reap.

This book will be the catalyst of a movement that will unite black men not only in America but across the globe. "When Men Lean In We All Win" will bring a unity to our brothers across the diaspora that will bring the type of hope, motivation and drive that will ignite the God in all of us and restore us as the black race, the original man in PEACE and LOVE.

PREFACE

R. Wesley Webb

In this COVID-19 environment it has provided an opportunity for reflection on how we as Black men can best make a difference to impact our communities; in raising our families, pursuing our careers, and giving back to influence the next generation on how to be their very best.

This compilation of stories will showcase some of the men that are seeking to make such a difference. By them giving their perspective on how they dealt with adversity and staying the course in pursuing their goals, it will inspire and give insight into their character.

The themes of the compilation include revitalization, education, and representation which are key factors in driving success. In revitalization there is a focus on communities and the possibilities of implementing real change that would benefit all families as whole. These changes may include new industry, home construction, and a significant investment in education, these are just a few of the factors that indicate a community that is ripe for growth.

In order to have a thriving community we must have suitable resources to bring in teachers, professors, and technical instructors. The ultimate goal would be not to leave anyone behind who has a genuine desire to do better for themselves, and having a well-funded educational base which will translate into; better jobs, upgraded community amenities, and a better quality of life. Education is the great equalizer in making lasting change and is something that is echoed by parents who encourage their children to; study hard, make good grades, and be ready for when opportunities come.

The opportunities lead to success and the best way to showcase this is through representation. As the saying goes, "success breeds success", and those that are so fortunate can serve as an example to others as what to do in preparing for that new job, creating that business start-up, or working on getting that promotion. In conceiving the goals, engaging men that are featured in this compilation would serve as a great resource in representing what success looks like. It is essential that our youth see such men in the community to give them inspiration for what they may aspire to become.

The contributors for this compilation come from various backgrounds and have a myriad of experiences which created a real opportunity for them to learn from one another and grow. This allowed for a greater degree of deference for the accomplishment of the men and the challenges they overcame to reach the current stage in their lives. These factors cannot be understated and by them sharing their stories, it is a form of giving back to the community to help those who are currently in a similar job or business. No one in the world makes it on there own and the gift of knowledge is worth its weight in gold because it fuels the potential for the success that we all seek.

As black men we're all a part of the brotherhood; which is very special, no matter where we come from the universal nod, or giving dap as a greeting is always understood. The bond is what drives us to be the best that we can be in striving for success and the opportunity to make a difference by blazing a new path for others to follow. Therefore, when we as men lean in, we all win.

FOREWARD

AWARD-WINNING COMMUNITY LEADER / ACTIVIST

THE HONORABLE CARL O. SNOWDEN

Black men speak. Black men write. Black men matter. Dr. Larry White, Sr. has gathered a group of African American men to tell their stories in their own voices. The voices give definition and meaning
to *When Men Lean In, We All Win*. This book captures the stories of African-American men in the 21st century. Each story is unique and yet the hue of each of the writers makes these stories interesting and powerful.

As you read the wisdom, wit, and insights contained in the chapters, remembers you are reading about Black men, who leaned in and made it possible for us all to win.

Carl O. Snowden,
Author and Activist

DR. LARRY WHITE SR.

WHEN MEN LEAN IN
We All Win
REVITALIZATION, EDUCATION, & REPRESENTATION

DR. LARRY WHITE SR.

THE SIGNIFICANCE OF BLACK MEN IN THE HOME: LEAVING A LEGACY

As The Visionary Author of this amazing compilation of phenomenal black men soon to be *Bestselling Authors,* I am very proud to be leading this project. I personally hand pick these successful black men that are not only great in business but also they give back to their communities. I have the honor and privilege to learn from these men during tough times as we bond to together during a Pandemic called COVID-19. My Chapter will focus on the significance of black men in our homes. Statics show that it is more likely for black men to be incarcerated at a higher rate than other ethnicities if they are not a part of a two parent house-hold. My chapter will focus on when black men are present chances are greater for success. Since the murder of George Floyd, systemic racism is at an all time high in our country. This has been a generational issue for black men for decades. We can no longer as black men, allow past behaviors be a blueprint for our future. As young man growing up in an urban area in Northwest Indiana, I had my fair share of challenges, success and failures as I matriculated through school and sports. I had a Father who instilled education in me from the beginning. He was also a great husband to my mom and they were married for 39 years. He spent countless of hours with me at the park and we had long talks about family values, sports, and education. He was my role model my entire life and kept me grounded by playing sports and taking me to the library every day during the summer. He was a Navy Veteran and ultimately became an electrician as a civilian and retired with over 35 years at the same company.

My dad rarely missed a day of work and exemplified integrity to our entire house-hold. After graduating high school both my older brother and I joined the Navy following in our Fathers footsteps. We were both very successful in the U.S Navy serving our country and received numerous accommodation medals and awards. I have been afforded the opportunity to have travelled the world three times over and the most important thing in life is family. Seeing my parents being married was also a great example of my Father providing for our family and always being there. I have been married for 18 years to my beautiful wife and try to immolate my dad by being the best dad I can be to my children. Being present is vital to our young black men today more than ever especially as a black father during a Global Pandemic. I have had my ups and downs in life as most of us have, but I have been able to focus on family values that my dad instilled in me to get through tough times. As black men, we must go a step further in our homes and Corporate America preparing our sons for diversity and being competitive in the work space. It all starts at home; a strong foundation will equip our young men to be confident and affirm leadership roles as they get older. I am the proud Father of three amazing men. I tell them everyday how much I love them and to aim high in efforts to achieve their goals. My oldest son Larry is a graduate of Radford University and is currently working in Corporate America as a Marketing Director in Washington, DC.

When Men Lean In, We All Win. The entire family wins. As black men and black leaders, we must focus on Economic Inclusion in our communities.

Once the development and implementation of Economic Empowerment is disseminated throughout the country for minority communities then we stand a chance in the Revitalization, Education, and Representation of our generation. In the words of Fredrick Douglass *"It's Easier to Build Strong Children, Than Repair Broken Men"*.

****

Let's change the narrative of this quote for the younger generations to come, the Millennial's, Generation Z. and Generation X. Be the difference they want to see!

Now let's take a look at our subtitle in three areas:

- **Revitalization**

  As we look at many Black Communities being gentrified today, we must take a stance in revitalization in urban areas across the country. We must invest our money into our communities like Black Wall Street in effort to increase economic inclusion for Small Business Owners. I am firm believer in money changing hands multiple times in the black community; it should not stop at the first hand!

- **Education**

  A good friend once told me that "Education is The New Sport". Meaning let's teach our youth to become lawyers, school teachers, judges, entrepreneurs instead of just being an athlete as the only way to success. Often times when sports are no longer an option for the individual and with no education to fall back on, this becomes a stigma of misrepresentation of athlete with no back-up plan. We must instill in our youth that an education, trade or a business certification is the first option in order to lay a solid foundation for general wealth, finance, and a longtime corporate career.

- **Representation**

Being represented in the Community, Home, Church, and Corporate America are vital ingredients in order to make progress and witness change. We must be present in our homes illustrating hard work on a daily basis; being the first role model they see! My dad always instilled me to be on time and show up with integrity. Knowing your WHY is very important in becoming successful, and being competitive in the Global Market in the 21st Century with cutting edge technology. Representation requires being present and making an impact in the work place and all aspects of your journey to success. It's not what they say when you are IN the room, it's what they say when you are NOT in the room. My experience as business owner for the past several years has been finding my niche and perfecting it which eventually leaves a lasting impression on clients, customers, and colleagues.

As a black business owner, I have been afforded the opportunity to have received The President's and Dream Keepers Awards from the NAACP. Two of the highest awards you can receive for Community Service and Leadership. My mom was in attendance that night and I remembered the look on her face as I cross the stage. She always taught to strive for excellence and dream as a black man. A year later, I would go onto receive Entrepreneur of the Year at the Spirit of A Dove Black Tie Gala earning recognition in the Baltimore Sun and Washington Post. These opportunities have never come into fruition without a strong foundation at home and Faith in Jesus Christ.

I am truly humbled by these opportunities but there is much more work to be done. I am currently serving as Chairman of the prestigious DMV Mastermind Group. This group has a focus on community outreach such as Feed the Homeless Projects, Voter Registration Drives, Business Development, and Entrepreneurial Empowerment. Given back to our communities is a must. We must all lean in with a purpose especially men to our youth with unapologetic determination of reaching our goals. This makes my fourth book with a concentration on penetrating communities like never before. As I write this chapter several black men and women are dying daily due to COVID-19, and senseless killings by police officers. My heart is heavy and I want change because as a black man, I am compelled to win this race. The race for equality and legislation that is suited for African- Americans. I will continue to do my part by using my platforms to disseminate positive message on my Talk Show and Social Media.

My Podcast Airs each Thursday at 10:00 AM EST on all Social Media outlets. I use my platform to give others a voice and opportunity to share their vision and goals. In 2020, especially during the Pandemic my show has had a concentration on Voting, Black Lives Matter, Social Injustice Issues, and Empowerment. Most of my TALK Show Guests are Life Coaches, Authors or Entrepreneurs with a mindset to make change in their own communities. I encourage all leaders to use their platform to invoke change in today's world of Chaos. My motivation in life is simple. It is merely to operate in excellence and help others grow into their maximum potential. Your journey in life is not always your destination. There will be times of struggle and pain but having faith in God will push you through the pain and position you to your purpose! The ability to use your God-given talents are key in reaching your full potential in life and your goals need to be in alignment with God's plan for you and your business. Often, we try to accomplish things on our own, but never realizing to pray about your initiative before execution. It is important getting a clear understanding from God on his will for your life, family and business endeavors.

I would not be writing this book if I did not hear a message from God asking me to execute this mission. He knows who will benefit from reading this book. It is my responsibility to listen to God, so that I can reap the harvest of being an obedient servant to his Holy Kingdom. The ability to work together as a functioning group takes perseverance, patience, and faith. Faith allows us to stay committed while on the journey until the blessings come down. The Lord will often say "yes" to our prayers, he will often say "no" and will often say "wait". In order to receive the true abundance life, we must listen to God's voice and be in alignment for his blessings. Many times, when you plant bad seeds in your life, you can't fully experience your true blessings because you can't recognize the blessings do to the negative seeds planted. It is imperative to plant and sow spiritual seeds in efforts reap the spiritual gifts that God has planned.

I am reaping the true benefits of God's great based on the seeds I have sown over the past thirty years. I am overjoyed to publish my fourth manuscript as I know it will inspire many people and generations. The ability to reach other people by way of books, events, workshops, and seminars is my passion with bottom line results of seeing my mentees and colleagues benefit from my wisdom and tutelage. I know this book will inspire community leaders and activist to be even more involved more than ever, to be better and do better! I am constantly reminded of Operating in Excellence at all times in the sole efforts in assisting people to cross over to greatness using their own power. During this horrific time of COVID-19, I will continue to demonstrate positive behaviors and leading by example. I am blessed to use this book to **Motivate**, **Educate**, and **Inspire** all people to reach greater heights within their own lives.

In 2017, I was on my first business tour called Deposit Your Dreams into Success; I used a catch phrase with hashtags called #BeInspired #BeEmpowered #GetConnected. I remember how nervous I was thinking no one would show up. God assured me people would be in the seats and that was his way of stretching me and testing my Faith. The tour would go on to be a huge success; I was leaning into my truth. My mission during the tour was to simply empower communities around the country with the sole purpose to revitalize and strengthen small businesses. After visiting Newark,DE. Chicago, Illinois, and Atlanta, Ga., I could see and witness the impact my team and I were having.

The tour was also used as a spring board for programs and my first book called "The Ultimate Networker & Entrepreneur. Empowerment is very important to me as a business owner; it serves as an accountability measure for our goals and determination in completing a task. Being held accountable as a leader is key in business because it allows you to gain confidence in personal development and growth. I would like for our readers to take ownership of their passions and create that seat at the table and being able to have a voice at that table. Each day I wake up, I am filled with passion and empowerment to get me through the day. As leaders, we must figure out what motivates us to be great and go out and fulfill our dreams. I close with this, when empowerment meets inspiration you have Greatness! Never set your goals too low, believe it and you can achieve it with a mindset of success. One of my mentors told me to think 10 to 20 years down the line creating the pathways to generational success not only just for me but for my grandchildren and their families.

These 15 men in this book collaboration will change the narrative of the portrayal of black men in today's society as we continue to strive for excellence and equality for generations. This book will also illustrate the legacy of great men working together to change lives!

We will be different, we will act different, we will roll different but most importantly, we will make

The Difference!

-Dr. Larry White, Sr.

www.vipeventsconcierge.com

DR. LARRY WHITE SR.

Journal **N**otes

_____

_____

_____

_____

_____

_____

_____

_____

_____

_____

_____

_____

_____

_____

_____

_____

_____

_____

_____

_____

_____

_____

DR. WILLIAM D. SCOTT

TURNING POVERTY INTO
PROSPERITY

"How to make something from nothing"

Dr. William David Scott was born in Talladega Alabama in the desegregated south, 8 months before the assassination of Dr. Martin Luther King Jr., the seventh in the line of nine siblings, five sisters and three brothers. Given the middle name "David", named after King David in the Bible abstracted from the book of Psalms, by his aunt Katherine Inez Sawyer a noted gospel singer and musician, who knew that he would be blessed in the artistry of music and live up to King David name.

David, as referred to in his early years, began to sing in the choir at the tender age of five and was playing for the youth choir at the age of eleven. Upon entering high school Dr, Scott received formal piano lessons at Talladega College under the direction of Dr. William Garcia, and Dr. Roselyn Briethway later to become the musician for the Patterson Gospel Singers.

Relocating to Atlanta GA in 1985 upon graduation from Talladega High School, Dr. Scott embark on a thirty-five year career in the music industry that would take him to many corners of the world, allowing him to play for numerous groups, church choirs, concert choirs, college choirs, community choirs, military choirs, and soloist. Coupling his love of gospel music with that of R&B, Jazz, Blues, and Hip-Hop "Scotty" as referred to in his later years would embark as an International Personality around the world and enjoy the opportunity to share the stage with some of the best and well known talent in the music industry. Associate member of The

Academy of Music (Grammy365). Dr. Scott is a frequent on the Red Carpets, from the BET Awards to the Grammy's.

Dr. Scott's extensive career in the music industry was paralleled with his military and professional careers. He served 3 years in the United States Army Alabama National Guard and 12 years in the United States Navy. During his military career he was stationed on six commands in the United States and abroad in the London, United Kingdom, Gaeta Italy, and Toulon France. A highly decorated Desert Shield and Desert Storm Veteran with a wall full of achievements and earned over 30 Medals and Ribbons to include 2 Navy Achievement Medal, 3 Navy Unit Commendation, Meritorious Unit Commendation, National Defense Medal, 3 Good Conduct Medal, Armed Forces Expeditionary Medal, Southwest Asia Service Medal w/Bronze Star, Armed Forces Service Medal, Arm Achievement Medal, Liberation of Kuwait Medal, Army Service Ribbon, 5 Sea Service Ribbons, 3 Overseas Ribbons, Navy Marksmanship Ribbon, Expert Pistol Shot Medal and Enlisted Surface Warfare Specialist Pin.

Dr. Scott is a Management Consultant and alumnus of the very prestigious accounting firm Deloitte and Touché and has worked with several Top 100 Companies. He holds a Bachelor of Science Degree in Management from the University of Phoenix, Tech Degree in Information Systems from American Business and Technology University, a Master of Business Administration in Operations Management from American InterContinental University, a PhD in Organizational Management and Leadership from the University of Berkley, and a Doctor *"Honoris Causa"* in Music from Los Angeles Development Church & Institute.

If you think your life is nothing, you are missing out on something. To change your situation, you must get out of your own way. The only reason you are in the same situation is because you keep missing your turn. When you realize where you are going and you map out your destination, you will know when to go left, when to go right, or when to go straight ahead. Let me take you on a journey with a young man that was dealt a hand and how he played it.

MAP OUT YOUR DESTINATION

Life deals everyone a different hand, it is not what is in your hand, but how you play your hand. Just because your deck is stacked with low cards do not mean you will not make any books, the person with all the high cards do not always play their hand right. You must position yourself to win no matter what. Just because you are born into poverty do not mean you have to stay in poverty. Once you learn how to make something out of nothing, your poverty will lift you into prosperity.

PLAY THE HAND YOU WAS DEALT

My birth mother died when I was nine years old but my grandmother and the mothers of the community step in and made sure the mother figure continued to live. My father was not present in my life and there were eight more mouths to be feed. One may say that my deck was full of low cards, but thank God, I learned how to play my hand. There were times when I did not have much food but I wasn't hungry, there were times when I didn't have much clothing but I wasn't naked, and there were times when I didn't have much hope but I wasn't hopeless.

BE GRATEFUL

My journey is no different than hundreds of young black men and young women who were born into poverty. The only difference is the way I chose to map out my destination. Although it was popular and tempting to stand on the corner; drink, smoke, and gamble, I knew that was not my turn, so I kept straight. Although it may not have been popular to got to church three and four times a week, I knew that was my turn, so I turned right. That right turn would take me in a direction of spiritual gratification and life changing decision making.

DON'T MISS YOUR TURN

My plan was not to wallow in self-pity but to elevate my self-esteem. See there were others that were dealt a better hand, meaning they had the high cards. The mother and father were present in

DR. WILLIAM D. SCOTT

the home, they had plenty food on the table, they wore nice clothes, and appeared that they were winning the game. Seeing them enjoy all these high cards in their deck made me feel worthless, but because I took the right turn God made me understand that I was not worthless but **"worth it"**.

KNOW YOUR WORTH

I learned at an early age that if you want something you cannot get it by doing nothing. I began to walk the neighborhood to rake leaves and cut grass. I began to wash cars and run errands. I began to make my own money and buy my own clothes, not realizing that I was setting myself up for successes that I would have never imagined. I was developing work ethics at 9 years old, motivated to succeed at 10 years old and by the time I was 11 years old I was a young entrepreneur. I was learning my worth.

OPEN YOUR EYES SO YOU CAN SEE WHERE YOU ARE GOING

Now I see through a glass clearly, although I was dealt a low hand in poverty. If I play my hand right, I will prosper. Although playing sports in school was the hip thing to do, it was not the right turn for me, so I took a left turn into music. Music allowed me to imagine and create. It was something that could make you happy but sad, excited but calm, it can show you how to love and hate. It became the trump card in my hand. Out of all the low card in my hand, I was deal a card that would take me from poverty to prosperity.

KNOW WHEN TO PLAY YOUR TRUMP CARD

What I failed to realize is that while I was trying to figure it out, God had already worked it out. I was named David from the bible and the book of Psalms (*musician*). David was a shepherd boy **(poverty)** that would become a King **(prosperity).** He took nothing and made something. I do not think it was an accident that I would become a musician like David. Music would be my trump card for the next 35 years, the one thing that would always keep money in my pocket, food on my table, clothes on my back, and joy in my heart. The talent did not cost me ***nothing,*** but music was ***something*** that everyone needed in the good and the bad times.

So, you could say that the right turn I took for spiritual guidance and the left turn I took for music aspirations would put me on a straight path to be successful. Because music was such a powerful trump card, I coupled it with everything that I did in life from my military career to my professional career.

The 3 P's to Prosperity

Pride, Perseverance, and Prospective Character = Prosperity

PRIDE – Take pride in all that you do, not matter what it is. You will make many wrong decisions before you make the right choice. No matter what job you do be the best at what you are doing, just always know that you are preparing yourself for greatness. You are somebody because you are present.

PERSERVERANCE – You will fail! But long as you are willing to get back up and try again you will succeed. See failure is designed to keep the black man down, because it puts you a place of worthlessness and pity. Let your personal testimony be, not how you fell, but how you got up.

Prospective Character – Only you can control your destiny. You are the leading man or woman and have the leading role in shaping an entire generation. Once you get in touch with yourself, you can touch the world. Your character matters and how you treat others will be a testimony of your gratefulness.

PROSPERITY

God will not bring you to it if he is not going to bring you through it. Your success depends on you deeds, if you do not put nothing in you will not get nothing out. If you sow your seed now you can enjoy your crop later. **(RETIREMENT)**

<u>Journal Notes</u>

_____

_____

_____

_____

_____

_____

_____

_____

_____

_____

_____

_____

_____

_____

_____

_____

_____

_____

_____

_____

_____

_____

_____

DION BANKS

DEAR ANCESTORS...I HEAR YOU

I dedicate this chapter to the seven generations of my lineage who came before me, suffered for, fought for me, prayed for me, and died for me. The blood that runs through my veins carries not only your DNA, but it also embodies your strength, courage, resilience, and tenacity that makes me who I am today. I am a strong black man who is dedicated to carrying on your legacy by following in your footsteps of greatness.

I decided to begin my journey with this chapter at the water front in Cambridge, MD. A small quaint town on the Eastern Shore of Maryland. Cambridge is known mostly for its scenic waterfront views, seafood, and Harriet Tubman, and American abolitionist, nurse, spy, and political activist. I've decided to provide a view of our great city through my lenses as a black man growing up in America with a strong to my roots. Sitting here on the water front is where the story of my life documented life begins. I say document because my story begins with my ancestors being stolen from Africa seven generations. My African Culture and history were one of the first victims of the transatlantic slave trade. I will share my family's experiences from slavery to freedom and how their spirits and energy guide me today to carry on and be a productive black man in a world where we are still not fully excepted as equal.

To give you some historical perspective, Cambridge was settled by English colonists in 1684 and is one of the oldest colonial cities in the state of Maryland with the second deepest water port in the state. During the early colonial period, Cambridge was known as a port town with their primary goods to trade being wood, tobacco and mixed farming, all worked by slaves. While cotton wasn't king during the early days of Cambridge and we did not grow cotton on the Eastern Shore, Cambridge would play a major role in the supply and demand of slaves as the laws change and the demand for slaves in the south became more frequent. In 1793 the cotton industry was revolutionized by the Cotton Gin, engineered by Eli Whitney in 1793. While this invention was a game changer making it easy to separate cotton fibers from their seeds, it was the catalyst that drove the darkness of slavery to it most volatile peak. To meet the demands of this new cotton separation technology, you needed more bodies to pick the cotton. In 1807, The Act Prohibiting Importation of Slaves was enacted and took place in January 1, 1808. This is when slave owners would search the eastern states to purchase slaves in bulk to send south. Life on the shore for the enslaved was often filled with fear of separation due to the demands for bodies in the south. Faith in knowing the atrocities of slavery would end one day was enough to remain hopeful that someday their children or their children's children, would not have to endure the brutality of slavery.

In 1802, my fifth-great-grandfather Samuel Green was born into slavery around 1802. Unlike many other enslaved men and women, he did receive some education and was a licensed exhorter in the local African Methodist Episcopal Church. Even though he was still enslaved, he became a prominent man in unifying other free African Americans in the community. In 1832, Green's owner, Henry Nichols dies in 1832, bequeathing him his freedom five years later. He worked diligently to pay off remaining four years of payment due for his services and was able to purchase the freedom of his wife for $100.00. Even though he was able to purchase his Wife's freedom, their two children remained slaves for life as written into law. Now a free man and disgusted with the evil of slavery, Samuel Green played a role in the Under Ground Rail Road and was known to have been in contact with Harriet Tubman as she made several trips back and to Dorchester County to assist slaves with their journey to freedom. In 1854, his son Samuel Green Jr. ran away to Philadelphia where we later met William Still, a conductor on the Under Ground Rail Road and best known for documenting the runaway slaves who arrived in Philadelphia. His daughter Susan, my fourth-great-grandmother was sold off to a slave owner in Missouri. My fifth-great-grandfather would continue his fight to end slavery. In 1855 he attended the National Convention of the Free Colored People of Maryland in Baltimore to resist the encouraged migration of blacks in the United States back to Africa. Now a free black man with a voice and standing up to systematic oppression, attention to his actions were high and all local eyes were on him. In March 1857, eight slaves from Dorchester County, Maryland escaped following a route provided by Harriet Tubman. Their names were Henry Predeaux, Thomas Elliot, Denard Hughes, Lavina Woolfley, James Woolfley, Bill Kiah, Emily Kian and one other person. (I think it's important to call out their names). Samuel Green provided them with instructions that he received from Harriet Tubman. Green was now under surveillance by the local authorities who were looking for any reason possible to arrest him. That day surely came on April 4, 1857 when he was charged with knowingly having an abolition pamphlet called "Uncle Tom's Cabin". On May

14, 1857 he was sentenced to 10 years imprisonment in at the Dorchester County Courthouse which still stands today and has what they refer to as a bandstand, but historical records show that is where the slave auction block was once located, meaning my fourth-great-grandmother was likely sold on that very spot. Five years later, Green was freed under one condition, he had to leave Maryland. He and wife Kitty emigrated to Canada. After the Civil War, they returned to back to Dorchester County where he became an active member if the Delaware Conference of the African Methodist Episcopal Church with a focus on education and religious instruction. He later got involved in the Centenary Biblical Institute in Baltimore that focused on training young men for the ministry. This would later be called Morgan State University. He later moved to Baltimore to be close to his work and died there on February 28, 1877. After slaves were freed in 1865, my fourth-great-grandmothers daughter, my third-great-grandmother Jennie Nichols who was born in Missouri, migrated back to Dorchester County with a Bible in-tow, with hand-written documentation of my family's routes.

My fifth-great-grandfather embodies the title of our book eloquently, "When Men Lean In, We All Win". Knowing the I am the product of a man who was stripped of his freedom, culture and labeled a slave for life but defied all the odds by challenging a system and staying true to his African Methodist Episcopal faith give me the power the strength to do all things. One thing that is often missing in the African Community is a lack historical knowledge about our own ancestry understanding of what our people had to endure from Jamestown 1619 with documentation of the first slaves in our country, to the atrocities of slavery until 1865, the passage of Black Codes in 1865, followed by Jim Crow laws and Civil Rights. Even today, 401 years after the arrival of the first document slave in the United States, we are still suffering in many ways and being marginalized, disenfranchised and overlooked. I often wonder how different our young brown boys and girls growing up in this country would act if they really understood the true totality of Black Lives Matter and when the movement truly started. I believe this could be the motivator for them to take control of all black and brown communities in our country by focusing on education, representation and revitalization. Educating our own kids to let them know that it was slavery that build this country yes, but it's now time to build our communities. We do this but filling their minds with our ancestral history. We show the leadership live time by being constantly present in our communities and have a seat at EVERY table where decisions are made that effects our communities. We teach them about black wealth and the importance of having business in the communities and the power of having the dollar flip within our communities before it leaves. Together we can create the change in the world we want to see. Our future of success starts with us understanding our past to building a strong foundation for our future generations to stand upon. It all starts with collaborations like this…

"When Men Lean In, We All Win".

<u>Journal Notes</u>

_____

_____

_____

_____

_____

_____

_____

_____

_____

_____

_____

_____

_____

_____

_____

_____

_____

_____

_____

_____

_____

_____

WAYNE TAYLOR

REFLECTIONS: COVID-19

Having been blessed to be raised by two hardworking, loving, and religious parents and the youngest out of seven kids, I didn't know anything about hand me downs nor did I ever miss a meal. My dad worked two jobs (employed by the federal government and private retail), one overnight and the other part-time in the evenings. I was born in Washington DC in public housing. In 1962, we moved to Prince Georges County, four years after my birth, because daddy saved enough money to buy three-quarters of an acre of land and built a 4 bedroom house (we still own the house today)in a small town called "Little Washington". Yes, it was in the middle of white-owned developments and only African Americans lived there, surprised by the name? Most of the residents didn't have running water so I always thought we were rich.

Growing up in then, rural, Prince Georges County was beneficial because the educational system was growing and so a new school was built within walking distance of our house. Although my sisters and brothers attended mostly segregated schools, I was fortunate to attend integrated schools. In 1972, the Prince Georges County Board of Education voted to balance the school by invoking "Busing!" So instead of attending high school fifteen minutes from my home, I was bussed 45 minutes to Surratsville Senior High in Clinton MD. The school was majority white but we got along very well. It was during this time, I got my introduction to politics and the political process. In my senior year, I was elected to the Student Government as the President. Part of the curriculum each week was spent working as a page for the City Council members in the County Seat of Upper Marlboro. The entire experience of high school was very beneficial for me because it shaped my broad interpretation of America. Although my understanding of society was of learning about the Civil Rights Movement, The Black Panthers and what it meant to be Black in America, having had the opportunity of being educated with a majority of white faces, enhanced my understanding of the opportunities in America (or so I thought.)

Upon graduating, I started working and it took a few years to find my nitch. As an Insurance salesman, I began my many years of volunteerism. First as a Cub Scout Leader, PTA President, and Sunday School Teacher. Leaving the field of insurance and taking a position with a Not-For-Profit in Washington DC, I became a mentor for low-income kids in Southwest while managing an after-school program. During the height of the Crack Epidemic, I volunteered to become a member of the Youth At Risk program. Several of the youth were part of the correctional system but the majority were from low-income, broken homes and casualties of the detriment caused by Crack Cocaine, in it's beginning. After spending twelve days in the mountains of Pennsylvania, ten adults and ten youth came back to Washington DC feeling "we have bonded and over the next twelve months, we are going to demonstrate CHANGE. This was the early nineties and several of the youth went on to college, while others melted into society.

Upon leaving the Not-For-Profit, a property management company in DC had a Social Services arm to which I became a Community Engagement Coordinator. My first assigned property was Frederick Douglass Homes in Southeast Washington DC. One of the greatest accomplishments there was teaching the kids how to become salespeople. During the after school program, we became engaged in a conversation on "what I want to be and naming someplace I would like to go." Most of the kids wanted to visit Disney in Orlando and so the conversation turned to, how do we get there. In the end, we talked about how do we start to raise the money to go to Orlando. They became intrigued when told them about having a fruit sale. The kids sold boxes of oranges, grapefruit, and tangerines to raise enough money for a five-day vacation in Orlando. Out of that experience they learned about selling, marketing, and presentation, all tools needed to approach life as young adults. As my retail career climbed, my volunteer availability decreased.

I mentioned earlier that I was a Sunday School teacher but also a church youth organizer, Church Deacon and as a youngster, a mind-changing experience that introduced me to becoming a minister. I wanted the ministry to be on my terms, not proclaiming the goodness of God from the pulpit but working in the community "doing good." God allowed me to move about doing good but for years I suffered for turning my back on him. To me, I became Jonah in the belly of the Whale. Many of you know the old testament of Jonah, having been told by God to go to Nineveh to preach the gospel, Jonah went in the other direction to Tarshish. Jonah boarded a ship, a storm arose and the crewed tossed him into the water. The whale swallowed Jonah and spewed him onto the land of Nineveh. Many of us are like Jonah, we struggle to do it our way. Eventually, I arrived in Annapolis MD.

Upon arriving in Annapolis, my Purpose became so much more evident. I was elected, City Councilman, and knew my goal of "doing good" was back on track. Without thinking about what God had done for me (getting elected), I thought about more money and elevation. Not wanting to wait on God, I fell again! Starting from the bottom again is very humiliating but if viewed (outside of your context) can be very educational. Again, I was working for a Not-For-Profit, getting my undergraduate, and moving forward. Doing my tenure here, using stimulus funds allocated by President Barack Obama, the agency CEO asked me to work with the Project Coordinator to put together a summer jobs program. Putting our heads together, we came up with the Summer Green Jobs program. We put over twenty youth to work that year, that were recruited through the Anne Arundel Public School System. The program has been successful in achieving its goal, helping young people see themselves differently regardless of their circumstances. After that first year, I returned to retail management. My time for community engagement continued, I became a member of the Anne Arundel County Area Agency on Aging Advisory Council and the Chairman of the Commission on Aging for the City of Annapolis. Politically, I asked and was accepted to the Anne Arundel County Democratic Central Committee.

After reading "The Purpose Driven Life" by Rick Warren, it became confirmed that my life's journey wasn't over but was just beginning. Many ask me "when are going to retire" and response is "when I drop!" While driving for a Black Sedan Company, I'm engrossed in completing my MBA. Every day was a brand new opportunity to make a difference while yet enjoying the sunshine, then along came 2020.

The year started great and things were moving along until March 15th, when everything suddenly stopped. A virus called COVID-19 was affecting the nation and we all had to stay in our homes. I continued to engage our seniors by taking them for their errands, while both of us were protecting each other (wearing our mask.) I saw this as an opportunity to move forward on life long dreams. As a younger man, starting an organization dedicated to " making a difference in the lives of people" was the substitute from, becoming a pulpit preacher. You see, the mission of Jesus Christ was out amongst the people making a difference, for them, to gain the truth. Our mission, whether we accept it or not, is to be like Jesus! He left the blueprint for us to operate in daily lives, fulfilling his goodness. Even though he died, the fulfillment of his work continues. Dr. Martin Luther King was quoted saying "If a man (woman) hasn't found something to die for, he isn't fit to live." Every day of my life could be my last but every day I have will spent working to progress others. So during the pandemic, I started my corporation called "What's "Really "Going On!" Sounds familiar? Marvin Gaye brought this song to life and the words are even more apparent today. This benefit corporation gives me the ability to be a consultant and on the other side write grants to secure funds "to do good." Hopefully, through this vehicle, the best is yet to come, which will be "Legacy." Stay tuned!!!

G. ALFRED PALMER

THE POWER TO TRANSFORM A

GENERATION

We live in a culture where medicine has become a vital part of our overall existence. We have a potion, lotion, prescription fill, and pill for almost everything. They aid many in being able to function proficiently and productively. CVS stores outnumber almost all other franchises in many cities. They are located on almost every corner, and until lately, many were open 24 hours a day, seven days per week, depending on its location. What if I told you, I have a pill that you could take and that pill is guaranteed to improve and increase your mental acuity? It would maximize your physical health. It would also improve your ability to experience quality and transformative sleep and relaxation. Finally, it would add more productive years to your life. Would you take that pill? How much would you pay for it? There's a possibility to have all the above-mentioned without even taking a pill. It can be found in your individual purpose, because knowing purpose would guarantee clear thinking. Much of what we suffer from is due to stress, and knowing your purpose would relieve much of what you stress about; money, significance, success, provision, productivity, prosperity, promotion, etc. As a result, our physical health would improve. With less stress, we'd be able to sleep and rest more deeply, and quietly. Finally, all these above factors in our lives, we would arbitrarily add more quality years onto our lives. With those results as real possibilities, over the past decade or more, I have been focused in one direction.

Everywhere I go whether it be in a restaurant, hotel, shopping, almost anywhere. I ask purpose-hinged questions. It's allowed me to meet all types of people, which have allowed me to surmise the answers come from three types of mentalities. A purpose question might sound like this. "Do you know what's your purpose"? Or, "Why were you born"? Another question might be, "Have you ever thought about why you're here?" The retorts may similarly come in this manner, "Yes, I know my purpose!" The next person, with a funny look on their face may perplexingly respond, "I think I know my purpose." Finally, the last one stares off into space and honestly, introspectively, and soberly admits, "I don't know my purpose." The ability to answer purposed-centered questions cures every ill we as individuals, communities, and cultures constantly encounter. Additionally, our desires for achievement, notoriety, accomplishment, success, peace, and wealth are all found in one word...PURPOSE!

In your opinion, what makes your life worth living? What's worth getting up in the morning? Is it your job, family, or paycheck? Many people don't really have an authentic personal valued reason for getting up in the morning. The Center for Disease Control in a recently released study stated that; 1 out of 3 individuals have a heartfelt reason for getting up in the morning. That means most of us have no real authentic reason for getting up in the morning. Some would argue that just staying busy, makes life worth living, and all these things keep us busy. However, living a busy life doesn't equate to living a meaningful one. All of the above activities are actions, movements. But, not all action or movement is productive or purposeful. Action may be perceived as good movement and good things to do. But truth be told, not everything that's good is right. Just because something is good, you doing it isn't always the right thing to do. There will always be good things to do, but it doesn't mean its right, for you. We must come to a place of understanding that everything good isn't right, but everything right is good! Which points to the importance of finding the right thing to do opposed to a good thing. Purpose is the right thing to do.

Purpose is of immense importance. It's so important because it's the reason you were born. There's nothing more important than that! Its what makes one's life worth living and not merely existing? Mark Twain said, "The two most important days in one's life, is the day they were born, and the day they find out why". Discovering purpose has been proposed in many different veins, some say there's a strand or thread that's interwoven throughout our individual lives, it's called a seminal moment. These seminal moments present themes, connections, awakenings, and opportunities to find out the true reason why we are here, why we were born.

People who realized the seminal moment that tips the balance of the scale of their lives, lives of others, their culture, society, or generation are marked in our lives. Every person is confronted with such moments throughout their lives, while some realize them when they experience them, while others don't. History is marked by individuals like Rosa Parks, John Lewis, Madame CJ Walker, Mae C Jemison, and many others, who have set examples of the importance of embracing seminal moments, and contributed to the transformation of their societal and cultural landscapes. This power of the seminal moment is derived from a much greater and foundational source. This source is a much-maligned, ignored, and minimized origin. The source is called purpose, which gives us an internal reason for living. Purpose is the most important issue facing humanity, and some just take it for granted and fail to realize its importance. The above-mentioned people came to realize its importance and as a result, we know their names and their contributions to society.

Have you leaned in to consider a question or thought with total honesty? One you contemplated with openness, and a willingness to accept its answer? Have you experienced a fervor desire to know something, and with humility made up your mind to accept its revelation without question? Some may not take the above questions seriously, and glancing answers them nonchalantly and dismissively, unaware or concerned with their eternal importance. When asked purpose questions, some may quickly respond, "My purpose is to do God's will." "My purpose is to glorify God." "My purpose is to take care of my family." Or, finally "My purpose is my passion!" All of these are great answers, but are not purposeful responses and don't require much introspection or soul searching. Some answers may be from rote memory, conditioned responses, and rehearsed scripts taught to us by those who we respect and trust.

Everything that was created was created uniquely, there's nothing else in creation like it. Not even twins are the same. So, you are unique, and as being unique there's only one place to find the answer of purpose, and that's in the mind of the maker of it. Your purpose is more individualized than to glorify God or provide for your family. That's not individualized, its general and non-specific. Not only is purpose is individualized and specific, its the most individualized and specific thing on earth as it relates to you. In fact here is how to define purpose using an acrostic. The following portion was taken from my first book, Purposeology: The Science of Purpose. Rediscovering Why You Were Born! Available on Amazon.com.

PERSONAL

Your purpose is personal and cannot be taught, but caught. It requires us to glimpse into the unseen and unspoken, of self-rediscovery. It relates the personal importance you bring to your community, culture, and clan.

UNIQUE

On earth there's approximately 6.5 billion people, and not one of us possesses the same fingerprint. The fingerprint is a physical representation of the uniqueness of our divinely encoded purpose. Take twins for example, they're born in the same location, have the same parents, internally resided in the same place, and shared the same sustenance, and still they have totally unique fingerprints or purpose. No one is like you, nor ever will be. You're a divine masterpiece, with a secret sauce unmatched throughout creation.

REASON

The most honest and purposed filled individuals in the world are children. They possess an ability to believe and receive without question. We need to become like them regarding rediscovering our purpose. There's a reason you were born, and many will never find it, because they haven't unpacked loads of "stuff" that society, family, school, and religion have piled on top of them mentally. As a result they have lost the child-likeness of believing and have replaced it with medication. Some have lost their ability to connect to purpose, and need to uncover or rediscovered it.

PINPOINTED

Pinpointed speaks the strategic idea of your purpose. It isn't scattered but you are specifically design to authentically fulfill your purpose. There is a predetermined location or environment, where you can optimize your performance in this dimension. You are divinely designed toward optimal performance in a pinpointed environment. There's a space, location, time, and matter in which you function. Similar to a flower, you have to be in the right season, sunlight, temperature, and soil to optimize! There's a pinpointed type of location and season that harmonizes with your optimal frequency.

ONE

Everything has one purpose, but may have several functions. The functions of a thing may be freely used or misused by the one using the functions. Many confuse the function of a thing, with the purpose of a thing. Purpose isn't function, but purpose uses function to one end, to fulfill its design, mission and assignment. The function of a thing may be used properly, or misused that's called abuse or abnormal use. The most important thought to remember is purpose is the reason of a thing, and its function is the energy that must be driven by rediscovered purpose and not by functionality.

SPECIFIC

The specific nature of purpose is critical because it allows the individual to remain focused and locked in on doing what's right as opposed to doing that which is good. It's easy to get sidetracked by the whims and desires of others, but knowing individual purpose solidifies one's direction and establishes boundaries. Boundaries that ward off good things for specific things that are right.

EXISTENCE

Purpose is the reason for your existence, and that existence is critical to bringing forward the very thing encased inside of you. You are a gift to the world. You're a very special gift that comes once in a lifetime. No one else can bring what you bring, or ever can do what you're to do in the manner you were created. You have something to contribute that no one else can. You are not a mistake, or worthless. You hold tremendous value, and that value came by virtue of your birth!

CLOSING

I want to ask you a question, and I want you to really ponder over it. It's important because this is your seminal moment. If no one has ever asked you this question before, you are left without an excuse from this day. My question is "Why Were You Born?"

CALL TO ACTION

If you have no idea, we can assist you in your journey and help point to specific signs of demarcation for you to find the You That Always Was! Go to gapalmer.com for more information.

Journal Notes

VINCENT LEGGETTE

BLACK FAMILIES MATTER:
INSPIRING MEN INTO ACTION IN
TROUBLED TIMES

"*If there is no struggle, there is no progress. Those who profess to favor freedom, and yet depreciate agitation, are men who want crops without plowing up the ground. They want rain without thunder and lightning. They want the ocean without the awful roar of its many waters. This struggle may be a moral one; or it may be a physical one; or it may be both moral and physical; but it must be a struggle. Power concedes nothing without a demand. It never did and it never will. (Frederick Douglass, 1857)*"

Leaning in to family

Within our African American families, education begins at home and is the first classroom children have. The family circle thus serves as the center for social, educational, economic, and spiritual life. We aim to build strong bonds among generations, and to pass on a way of life that has transcendent meaning. It is necessary, even critical, to have men leaning into this nurturing process.

My family has always had admirable men working hand-in-hand and heart-to-heart with phenomenal women. However, we know this dynamic is not present in all families, and particularly not within African American households. I don't wish to place blame on Black men for these shortcomings, or focus on the negative impacts of men's lack of presence in families and communities. My purpose is to lead by example, and to demonstrate through my family's traditions how "when Black men lean in, we all win" is more than a catch phrase. It's historical, contemporary, and prophetic.

I have personally benefitted from having strong, dedicated, and spirit-filled Black men lean into my life. Just one example is my dad, Charlie Leggett, who was deeply committed to his family, church, and community. He instilled those traits in me and my older brother Malcolm—and in turn, we have passed those values on to our families.

The legacy of my family and its philosophy of leaning in is intertwined with America's "peculiar institution," as slavery has been euphemistically known. Separating family was the weapon used by the small group to control and oppress the majority. My great-grandparents, Catherine McCall Graham and Sandy Graham, were born into slavery in Laurinburg-Maxton, North Carolina. At the age of 13, Catherine witnessed her family being torn apart through sales and trades. She vowed that when she became a woman and had her own children, she would do everything in her power to keep her family intact. Beginning in 1913, Mama Cathy started a tradition of bringing her family together on the second Saturday in August.

The family is the root of African American culture, and family reunions are what fortify those roots. The Black family reunion has the characteristics of a movement, as each year, more and more families hold their first reunion. We all feel that such important rituals have long contributed to the survival, health, and endurance of African American families, helping to maintain cultural heritage even in uncertain and turbulent times.

For many Black families, reunions are the most anticipated events of the year. My wife, my children, and I, along with dozens of other descendants of Mama Cathy Graham, always look forward to our annual gatherings. But 2020 has felt more significant because of the COVID-19 pandemic and the rise of "Black Lives Matter" positivity in the face of divisive attitudes fanned by "Make America Great Again" campaigning.

Continuing a 107-year tradition, the Graham Family Circle held its annual gathering on August 8, 2020. But because of travel restrictions and out of caution, we decided to use Zoom technology to keep the party going. We adopted the theme "Black Families Matter"—mindful of the global uprisings in protest of police brutality and injustices against Black and brown people, and in solidarity with the Black Lives Matter movement.

Black folks have always found a way to lean in and work around obstacles. For centuries, Blacks in Africa and the Americas used drum telegraphy to communicate with each other from far away. In the Antebellum South, drumming was banned because slaves were using it to communicate over long distances in a code unknown to their enslavers. Now, when our physically gathering together is being curtailed, we use electronic technology to maintain connections within the family—which feels even more vital during this period.

Leaning in to community

With many thanks to my strong family bonds, I have spent my personal and professional life in community service. My proudest accomplishment is getting off the ground a nonprofit

educational and environmental foundation. Starting with a vision and building a local legacy has happened because of my nature as a man to lean in for the benefit of others.

As a young boy growing up in East Baltimore, I was introduced to the Chesapeake Bay through weekend fishing trips with my dad. I caught the spirit of the Chesapeake through him—we felt the freedom that comes with being on the water, away from the asphalt and concrete of the city. I have roamed the expanses of the Chesapeake waterfront for more than 30 years, finding comradeship with the African American watermen I've met along the way. In 1984, I began the Blacks of the Chesapeake as a personal project, documenting these workers' contributions to bay history, industry, and culture.

I formally established the Blacks of the Chesapeake Foundation (BOCF) in 1999, with the mission of more widely sharing the legacy of African American achievement in the seafood and maritime industries; promoting the success of Mid-Atlantic seafood commerce; and conserving the bay watershed. BOCF's signature approach is utilizing pride in local history and culture as a gateway to engage underserved and non-traditional populations in environmental stewardship. The foundation's list of members and accomplishments smashes the myth that African Americans and marginalized citizens do not care about the environment.

The United States Congress and the Library of Congress recognized BOCF as Local Legacy Project in 2000, for bringing to light this little-known aspect of Americana. In 2003, Maryland Governor Parris N. Glendening commissioned me an "Admiral of the Chesapeake Bay," a lifetime achievement award for extraordinary commitment to the conservation and restoration of the Chesapeake Bay.

I also recognize the need for all citizens to lean in and push for legislative and judicial reforms. I am President and CEO of the Leggett Group USA., a consulting firm specializing in government relations, public affairs, and advocacy; and I am a Registered Lobbyist in the Maryland General Assembly. I have also answered the call to serve my community in leadership positions, including as a member of the Board of Directors of the Wiley H. Bates Legacy Center and the Chesapeake Legal Alliance, President of the Anne Arundel County Board of Education, and Chaplain for the Fire Department of the City of Annapolis.

The winner's circle

"Leaning in" is about wholeheartedly pressing forward toward a goal, and "winning" is arriving at a well- deserved victory. When men lean in, everyone around them wins. Their families prosper, their neighborhoods flourish, their communities are empowered, and whole nations are revived. It is my hope that every man accepts this personal challenge for greatness and stands tall in the center of his winner's circle.

Journal Notes

STEVEN LABROI

TEAM SPORTS EQUAL A LIFETIME
OF WINNING AS A BLACK MAN

I grew up playing team sports starting at 7 years old, which ended up as a blessing, growing up in a single parent household in Gary, Indiana.   Before organized ball, we played outside in the neighborhood all over the city back then crime amongst kids was not as bad. Once I reached seven years old my mother signed me up for organized sports through the local Pop Warner football league and Midtown Biddy Basketball leagues set up in our city for the youth by men in the city who wanted to give kids something to do. I don't even remember asking to play but this was the start of my rights of passage to manhood, mentoring, fathering, discipline, camaraderie, and where I learned team play. For a bunch of young boys, most coming from single parent households the discipline was swift and direct by the coaches who were policeman, Steel Mill Worker, Ex-Athletes, and men interested in the wellbeing of young men. All this, while some mothers watched during practice, while others worked seven days a week to provide this activity effectively keeping us off the street. During these times this was typical for your parent to provide this type of outlet especially since all the other children were participating and it allowed them to know exactly where you were during practice and game days. Our parents must have known that without this we could have been another statistic dead or in jail. This was growing up in the hood and little did we know it was the foundation of our entire lives and what was to come. What we did learn in our playing team ball is every young man the city of Gary at that time was some valuable life lessons, no matter where you lived in the city of Gary, Indiana - North, South, East or West in the city you came together to compete as youths and play to win – there were no participation awards it was either win or lose – a life lesson. Our shared experiences have proven to benefit us as men today as we are living and working in every endeavor of life across these United States and the World.

The guys I played with in organized sports are now grown men with families and real work experiences from corporate America, entrepreneurship, and blue collar uber success. They are family men with spouses and children of their own. Some of them have children who are super successful as well. After those adolescent years the guys split up moving to various school close to their homes and sides of town. I moved on to an all-Black High School Theodore Roosevelt built in 1929 for blacks with a rich history, where I excelled in academics, athletics and student government activities. All this from competing as a youth with the fellas in those leagues on Saturday and Sunday mornings I felt the need to compete at everything. Funny we then competed again against each another attending the different schools across the city of Gary.

Playing for some longtime rivals in Gary, Indiana we kept up some intense games on the field, on the court, and on the track, and still gave each other much respect after the heat of the battle knowing that we were all heading in the right direction – life lesson. I realized our lives crossed paths at a young age for a reason. When I left Gary to attend a Historically Black College - Morehouse College in Atlanta, Georgia I felt I was ready to leave home not knowing what to expect but knowing I had a great foundation. This was the college that the pastor of my home church attended graduating with the great Martin Luther King Jr. So, this was very exciting and comfortable because of the prestige of the school and also like my high school it was all black. An all black all male institution across the street from Spelman college an all-black all female institution surrounded by Morris Brown College, Clark Atlanta University formerly Clark College, and Atlanta University a separate graduate school now combined making up a center of black intellectual excellence and a central point to learn more foundation building skills in preparation for true adulthood. There I made even more friendships while studying my chosen field of business Finance and Banking. Also, ironically, the movie School DAZE by writer director Spike LEE also a Morehouse Alumnus was filmed on my campus during my years as a student (little did I know I would be an Executive Producer of a movie as well years later). It was a great time enjoying and studying at the AUC center in Atlanta, Georgia in the eighties. As the college years flew by I had no idea the universe would move me in directions that would all lead to my love for personal finance. Never forget your first thoughts and love of any particular subject or idea it is probably your gift from God to the universe. I always thought about why we did not have money and that I wanted to make sure I had money to help my mother since she worked so hard. We must take inventory of our life's dreams and not allow it to be pushed down by the noise of life and never let our true purpose shine.

Keep your hopes and dreams alive always. If it is his will it will be DONE!

So, being away from home for the first time in my life on my own forced me to make decisions I had not made before. When to get up, when to study, what to eat, when to do laundry, how to pay bills, how to operate as a man in real social and dating situations. The conscious mind of making my mother proud was ever present and always rang in my ear with thoughts in most all situations. This is what kept me on track to pursue my degree while learning and growing up in this new world. There are lots of hard lessons when you are in college; in your late teens and early twenties if you are away from home fulltime. It was also the very first time I had to learn to manage money on my own everyday where the consequences were directly affecting me daily. The major question was will I get my degree on time in four years while managing life on my own at this historically black college since it was real apparent that this was not just school it was new found friendships, a brand new social experiment (fun) and hard education that intertwined to impact your four years. There were some real distractions like parties, and road trips to other schools out of town. These distractions impacted me so much I finished in four and a summer with my Bachelor of Administration degree in Banking and Finance. The reality of it all is history but, is was painful at the time managing through wins and losses on your own. Yes, going through school and taking on my first real live employment opportunity after graduation I was forced to learn personal finance immediately since it was my education of choice as well. I did have some hard lessons like credit, collections, and judgments dealing with this new system of financial decisions. I tried my best to ask people and follow older friends, mentors, and coworkers to learn this thing called money management; but it seems like everyone did their own thing and would not discuss it too much. Again, remember none of my schooling from high school, college and even as a young adult did, I learn money management, but it was a source of my curiosity and angst since incomes were not very high during that time. You had to figure out how to make your money last for the month, paying rent, utilities, food, clothing, and happy hour with your friends. All these were the things young professionals did so you felt you needed to keep up. However, tracking and managing income and expenses were not the biggest priority and I definitely did not have any money management strategies or focus. But the universe was still pushing me in that direction without me knowing. I was able to survive by just knowing I was on my own and I had to at least cover food, clothing, and shelter or end up back staying with my mother. I felt manhood was at least having your own place to stay a car to drive and clothes to stay fresh when socializing.

So, finance became my way of life and my pursuit of learning personal finance has continued to grow. I have always figured out how to make money, since starting my working experience as a teenager all the way through college, income was a forgone conclusion. I have always held a job or a business all my life since my need to have my own money was strong. I just needed to figure out what to do with the money after I made it. Again, this was not taught in any school or at home although certain family members would always say "Pay Yourself First", which is a great sounding philosophy, but no one ever told me where or how to pay yourself. You realize quickly you are on your own and have to figure it out. There was so many distractions and products presented by banks, financial institutions, and investment professionals. It was confusing, so most of time I just spent the money on fun. No one gives you guidance or education as an adult to establish benchmarks and strategies you can adopt for yourself and your family. So, I realized one major strategy was to just pursue more and more money as if income was going to be the secret to the American dream. Keep getting new jobs get more education to get a better job and more money. You learn quickly MO Money Mo Problems. Bad habits with money at smaller incomes are the same habits you have at larger incomes nothing changes unless you change. I quickly learned later in life that WEALTH and assets are what we must pursue.

So life became a new frontier without the twenty-two guys on my Pop Warner football team to laugh with, talk to, and play sports with or the neighborhood brothers where we learned all things boys do in the hood good and even bad or even the ten guys on my Midtown Biddy basketball team where we played together and traveled together to different states to play teams all over the state and country. Also, without my coaches who guided my adolescence with discipline of hard practices and running our tongues out to exhaustion. I was left to figure it all out day by day. Oh, and yes, there was no Google or internet either; it was a very daunting task to figure out everything on my own.

As a single young man, I could hear the voices of my elders whose lessons rang loudly in my ear and as an older man it is the same today. However, I have used my education and experience to focus on learning how money works and also teaching others. My purpose has been found to help young African Americans learn money management and also helping my peers who had similar upbringing as myself correct the wrongs of the past which have become the habits of their present. Personal Finance is more important that making income, because no matter what income you make you must know how to manage it to create a life for you and your family. My nationwide strategy firm is my life's purpose and the universe has led me to this because I never gave up on my Dreams. I kept paying attention to my thoughts and not letting my failures and setbacks turn me back. They were life lessons from my foundation in Gary, Indiana all the way to today.

My non-profit Millennial Banking Concept a full 501c-3 organization reaches and teaches young adults personal finance. This to help change the situation I found myself in as a young adult essentially trying to "Figure" it out. Our program shows them how to "FIND" out that life and finances intertwine and that finances and cash flow is a constant and should flow from more than just income. It should flow from wealth and assets. We should teach them how to start building assets with ANY income and to build a financial foundation similar to the strategy in my book "Build Your Human Equity Line of Credit, Creating Assets in Any Economy".

My mission with my purpose is to help our culture see the real issues around building Life insurance policies (contracts) and strategies using these billion-dollar businesses. Black Lives Matter and I am fighting the fight from the inside. I will live my life correcting this miseducation.

My Life has been built on team sports, and the ability to build friendships with peers and adults, whom the life lessons are still with me today. I am actually still in touch with some of those guys and we continue to share in our past and current experiences, which is still a great way to learn how to manage life as it becomes even more complex moving into the future. Take an account of your life and all your experiences be thankful for each and every one of them. As long as you are living you can correct any mistakes and you can build on all the successes.

God Bless!

<u>Journal Notes</u>

_____

_____

_____

_____

_____

_____

_____

_____

_____

_____

_____

_____

_____

_____

_____

_____

_____

_____

_____

_____

_____

_____

_____

BRIAN KEITH BAILEY

ADAPTATION

My addition to this book is dedicated to my newly born grandson, O'ryan Laneil Keith Fedison. He added another strong male to the Bailey family. He is my Grand King! I hope my journey and my legacy inspires him toward greatness!

Brian Keith Bailey was born in Washington, DC and raised in Baltimore MD. He is a retired Air Force veteran and an entrepreneur. Brian is currently CEO of Bailey's Professional Service which provides real estate solutions for residents in the state of Maryland. As a real estate professional, Brian increased his presence by becoming a real estate author when he published the book titled, *Buying My First Home As A Military Veteran.* Brian's Entrepreneurial ventures also carries into the fitness realm as CEO of Fit Tyme Productions, as he is the author of the fitness programs

60

titled, ***The Mental Hurdle of Fitness Success System*** along with the workout DVD titled ***Chairaicize (Get Fit While You Sit)***. Brian recently partnered with his wife Sheila in teaching others the importance of detoxing and cleansing the liver, kidneys, lymphatic system, colon and blood with a program not only removed pounds of fecal matter and mucus from the body but also helps people experience more energy and weight loss. Their belief is disease starts in the colon and at the end of the day, your health is your greatest wealth.

Brian also has another powerful vision which is to create a nationwide resource and empowerment movement for dad's through his program called Dads of Determination which promotes fellowship and partnering efforts for fathers who are determined to be a force in the life of their children. Brian is married with three beautiful daughters and two amazing grandchildren. To learn more about Brian Keith Bailey visit www.briankeithbailey.com

The Beginning

My life started out by God making a way out of no way. It begins with my mother, the beautiful, smart and witty young lady from Westmoreland County Virginia named Kathleen Elizabeth Bailey (maiden name Thompson). After a visit with the doctor for vaginal spotting, the doctor recommended that she have a hysterectomy performed to clear up any problems she was having her with reproductive organs. Instead of following up with the doctor's suggestion, she decided to have another baby. At the time she had three kids, Clifford Thompson, Shirlene Thompson and John Bailey and the addition of one more was what she wanted before calling it quits. I guess she was bent on having a four-kid family. After finding out she was pregnant with a baby boy, it was discovered that her medical issue turned out to be Uterine Cancer. She waited for me to be born before beginning treatments. She was willing to sacrifice her life to save mine and in August of 1967, Kathleen left this earth leaving her newborn son to make it through life without the special guidance and love that only a mother could give.

The Transitions

My Aunt Nettie White (R.I.P – My mother's Sister) along with her husband (Everette) leaned in as they were my first saviors. These wonderful family members took me in even though they had a house full of kids. Their Bronx NY Apartment was barely big enough for their own family but they made sure that they made room for this cute little bouncing baby boy. My stay didn't last long as my second set of saviors, Aunt Allene Roberts, (My mother's oldest sister) along with her husband Charles Roberts leaned in by bringing me down to Baltimore to live with their three kids. Their kids were much older, so as the baby of the family, having me around as an infant, toddler, and kid that was full of energy was a test for her aging husband. You see, John Hopkins hospital did an evaluation on me and I was clinical diagnosed as hyperactive. I had the energy of three kids and it was too much for this family to handle. At the young age of seven it was time to move again.

Fostering My Way Through

This time my travels took me to the other side of West Baltimore where I moved in with a Foster family led by Mr. Wesley Foster who leaned in with his beautiful wife Annette. The memory of this transition stays on my mind as I frequently have flashbacks to the day when this bearded white man with a brown and beige shirt, brown pants and brown scuffed shoes pulled me away from my aunt and put me into his what I think was a Ford Pinto. I didn't know how to process this at the time but I remember not feeling scared. It was almost like my mother; my angel was helping me adapt. I remember when I met Mrs. Annette Foster, she was this nice lady who greeted me with a big smile as I was brought in the door with my assigned social worker. She wore a big smile a beautiful flowered patterned gown as she welcomed me to her home. Her house was filled with pictures that included a picture of Jesus in the kitchen (The Last Supper) and in the back yard they had two adorable dogs named Pepper and Peck! As the other foster kids came home from school or work, I knew I was going to be ok. From Doreen to Larry, George to Nadine to Mary to Bruce they immediately took me in as one of the family. I was enrolled into Lafayette Elementary school and remembered meeting teachers and administrators who would say, you are one of Mister and Misses Foster's boys right? The Fosters were respected in the community and in my opinion was one of the finest Fosters parents in Baltimore at that time. A lot of good memories came from that school to include watching a young Oprah Winfrey perform a one woman play and afterwards telling us kids that we could be anything we wanted to be if we set our minds to it. It's funny how those little memories end of being such a big part of who I became today. Thanks Oprah!

Between going to 7am Mass at St. Edwards Church and taking long rides to the country in that old brown station wagon with Mister and Misses Foster along with the other kids, my adaption to this family put me in a position better than many children who were placed into the system. You see, I learned that in order to make the best out of my life, I had to adapt. I could have sat around and pouted and I am not going to lie; I did have my down moments, but something inside of me said, your best days are coming. Get up, get moving and adapt!

Reunited

Finally, I was allowed to move back in with my biological family (Aunt Allene and Uncle Charles Roberts) at the age of 11. But it was a bitter sweet transition as I went from having a House full of my foster brothers and sisters and nieces and nephews to a situation where I was now the only child. It was bitter sweet as we were more than just foster kids, we were family. Even though we all had our own stories of how we got there, we all had to adapt to our surroundings and build upon our experiences in order to make it through life.

At this point I am growing up as the youngest of the family and basically the only child as all of my aunt and uncle's other kids had grown up and moved out. I had to adapt to my new school and the area. Even though I was back with real family, my transition did not turn out to be a bed of roses as I experienced bullying from some of the kids on the block. Not that I wasn't able to defend myself, but the constant harassing got to be too much for my Aunt and Uncle so off we moved to Baltimore County where I ended up finished my Junior and High School years and eventually joining the United States Air Force.

The men and women in my early childhood made a decision to lean in with the help of their wives. Each situation turned out differently but each occurrence made me stronger. The adaptation power that helped me overcome what may have seemed like a tragedy came from my heavenly angel (Kathleen). Her angelic assistance gave me the ability to adapt to many other things as I grew older. From losing my brother John Bailey due to suicide and soon after losing my oldest brother to HIV/AIDS, I realized that I had a gift when it came to the ability to adapt. This power has allowed me to be a beacon of light for all men who are going through or have been through situations and circumstances that may put them in a position where they wanted to quit, give up or cancel well laid out goals and plans.

A Brothers Love

My brother Clifford Allen Thompson was a man's man. He was well liked and was in my opinion was one of the smartest men on the planet. If we were able to register his IQ, I am sure it would have registered off the charts. I didn't meet him until 1980 along with my other brother John Charles Bailey aka Chucky. My biological sister Shirlene Thompson invited me to spend Christmas with her and her daughter in DC. This was a special treat because I would also get to meet my brothers for the first time. I met Shirlene earlier in my childhood while staying in the foster home but I only heard about having real brothers and during this Christmas being with my real brothers and sister became my best gift ever.

Clifford, immediately took me under his wing as big brother and made sure I was on the right track going from the journey of being a boy and learning how to be a man. We use to have heart felt conversations about everything from sex to career goals and even about how to approach life with a winning attitude with his saying, "Opportunities are Endless"!

Clifford was not perfect and I didn't care because he was my brother. He was a Vietnam Veteran with the street smarts of New York as he lived in the Bronx. But his street smarts lead to addiction. As the little brother, I always tried to find ways to help him move pass the addictions and become the superstar that I knew he could be. Eventually after I transferred from Hill AFB in Utah to my assignment back home in Maryland, I persuaded him to move down from New York to live with me. The only catch was, you must leave the drugs and alcohol alone and start working. Talk about rebounding! Not only did Cliff have a job, he had successfully found two well-paying jobs in the same area! The staff at both locations loved him and his work ethic but as he was making his ascension toward success, he soon found out it was only short lived as his body became infected with HIV/AIDS due to previously sharing a needle with another infected drug user. I watch this handsome and strong man become a shell of himself before my very eyes and after battling the disease he said to me, "Keith, I am so tired and I can't take this anymore. A few months later he joined my mother in heaven at the young age of 41. I had to adapt from this loss, as one of my leading cheerleaders left me as he transitioned to become another angel next to my mother but because of Cliff's leaning in with his words, action and love, I will always remember, "Opportunities are Endless". Rest in Heaven Clifford Allen Thompson.

A few years before the passing of my oldest brother, my brother John Charles Bailey committed suicide. I was on my way home from Anderson AB in Guam hoping to hang out and enjoy spending time with my brother when the call came in. Chucky as we called him was silent but smart. He suffered from depression and the loss of my mother affected him much more than it affected me as I was only 9 months when mom passed and he was 4. Chucky joined my mother in heaven at the young age of 24. Talk about having to adapt. Now both of my brothers were gone and whatever I decided to do with the rest of my life, it would have to be without my two big brothers to guide me through this journey called life. More are now angels smiling down on me and again I have no choice but to get up, get moving and adapt.

Fuel for the Journey

As I journey through life, I recognize these events could have killed me or lead me to believe that life is only meant to knock you down, so why try? But my journey has taught me to be optimistic in believing that in order to succeed, you have to find a way to adapt. You look for the good and learn from the experiences. The easiest route is to set back and say woah is me or you can practice effective adaptation. Do you think I wanted to be placed a Foster home? Was it fair to be raised without my mother? (not to mention I never found out who was my biological father). Was losing my big brother who was also my biggest cheerleader fair? The power to adapt to life's circumstances has giving me the reason to reach back and coach, empower and lead. My story is only a part of the collection of stories from other men but all of our stories resonate with someone searching for answers or guidance. I hope my adaptation story gives you the fuel needed for your journey through life. Get up, Get Moving and adapt!

If I can succeed, so can you!

Journal Notes

_____

_____

_____

_____

_____

_____

_____

_____

_____

_____

_____

_____

_____

_____

_____

_____

_____

_____

_____

_____

_____

ONDRAY JAMES

I AM NOT YOUR MISEDUCATED
NEGRO

Ondray James is a devout Christian, scholar, author, mentor, volunteer and a leader in his community. He is a husband and a father of three children. A native of rural Eastern North Carolina, he was born in the small town of Kinston. Ondray was a member of the historical 1998 Ayden-Grifton High School 4x100 Relay Track Team. His relay team broke the North Carolina 2-A class State record. Ondray has worked over 17 years as a Federal Acquisition professional; he has managed multi-million programs, awarded over 10 million dollars in federal contracts, and has worked with multiple small businesses to obtain federal contracts. He was nominated for Young Acquisition Professional of the Year from the United States Department of Agriculture. Ondray has always been a champion for small business owners and worked to increase small business participation in federal acquisition. Ondray has a B.S. in

Food Chemistry from North Carolina Agriculture & Technical State University and a M.S. in Nutritional Sciences from Howard University. He is a certified Federal Contracting Officer, Contracting Officer Representative, and Project Manager.

Hobbies: Fishing, Reading, Cooking

Goal: To strengthen and enhance the family structure by edifying and motivating men.

Purpose: To transition boys into productive men, husbands, and leaders.

My high-school had a strong culture of winning. My freshman and sophomore year, the varsity basketball team won back-to-back 2A State Championships. In four years, our varsity football team only lost 5 regular seasons football games. I was a member of the 4x100 relay team that broke the state record. At my school, all we cared about was winning and bringing home trophies. This culture fostered a championship mentality.

I learned very early in life that champions have an addiction to working hard. I really believed the success of our sports teams was that we "out worked" everyone. Yes, we had talented athletes; but we grinded in the weight room, studied hours of film and bought into coaching strategies. Practices were intense; conditioning was hard; and staying on the coach's positive side was challenging; but worth it. Being the best and winning championships was an addiction that we were willing to work hard to maintain. This may sound similar to the story of any championship team. However, we knew we were special because we broke records and won championships without basic facilities and resources. We broke the state 4x100 relay record, but we did not practice on a track, because my school did not have one. We trained on a grass Football field and practiced our baton exchanges by placing tape on the grass. We won without a track because the race started before we reached the starting line. We out worked everyone else in the state.

This mentality was ingrained in my psyche, so when I received a form about my plans after graduation, I considered my options from my championship perspective. When asked to select one of the following options:

a. Work- No educational plan
b. Military
c. Educational Plan-2 years at Community College
d. Educational Plan-4 year College/University

I proudly selected the letter "D," Educational Plan- 4 year College/University as my academic/career goal. I had spent years walking through the halls emblazoned with "Go Chargers!" The trophies in the cases had my name engraved into the gold. I believed I was college material, because I wanted to be a college student. I was in a state of disbelief and numb with confusion, sadness, and embarrassment when my guidance counselor told me that I was not college bound. She explained that the level of the courses on my schedule and my lackluster academic performance meant that I was not smart enough to attend a 4 year university. As I look back on that moment, I realize that the words of Maya Angelou are true:

I've learned that people will forget what you said, people will forget what you did, but people will never forget how you made them feel.

I am now 44 years old; yet I vividly remember the day my guidance counselor told me I was not smart enough to attend college. I remember thinking "That's not right. This is not fair!" I took the classes that my counselor and teachers recommended. I was always academically eligible for sports. I never missed school, and I did everything that was required. However, the system had not been designed to educate me. I was not being prepared for college. The system was designed to *miseducate* me so that I would only reach a certain level of success.

After I left the counselors office, one thought kept playing over in my mind "What if I work hard?" I knew I was smart, but I began to think about working harder and being smarter. The championship mentality I gained as an athlete was my lifeline. I ignored her advice, worked harder and applied to college anyway.

In 1933, Dr. Carter G. Woodson wrote "The Mis-Education of the Negro." In the book, Woodson explains the feelings of disillusionment many African Americans face in academic settings. He explores how African Americans were discouraged from exploring certain jobs and constantly told they were not fit to being educated. My guidance counselor was practicing the same strategy executed by her ancestors in the early 1900s; discouragement of professional education. To overcome this trauma, I had to answer the question that was replaying in my mind "What if I work hard?" I embraced the championship mentality to develop the "grit"; the ability to work hard and the confidence to believe in myself. I was born with a purpose and I was determined not to be a miseducated Negro because of the discouragement of a guidance counselor. I used the champion mentality to strengthen how I approach my education. I had to attack my classes as if I was training for a sporting event. I wanted to be the best student in the class which meant I must provide exceptional quality of work and produce "A"s.

I wasn't prepared for the arduous curriculum at North Carolina A&T State University. I needed to be committed and disciplined in order to be a successful college student. I had to embrace the challenges of learning new concepts and philosophies by taking time studying course materials and doing additional reading on the weekends. This championship mentality caused me to turn a 2.5 GPA my freshman year into a 4.0 by my senior year; but most importantly this mentality caused me to believe in myself in the classroom. My academic success fueled a passion for learning.

Shortly after my son was born, I attended Howard University. I didn't have the luxury of "chilling." I had to sacrifice watching my favorite sports teams play and hanging out with friends and family. I had to be intentional of my time and use the championship mentality to help me succeed. I rearranged my schedule; wrote research papers on the weekend and studied late at night, when my son went to sleep. Also, I used my vacation days to attend study groups and do my required reading. This lasted for about two years; but I knew if I kept sowing seeds by focusing my time on extensive reading, writing, and studying the harvest would be bountiful. I graduated from Howard with honors. Most importantly, I gained additional confidence in my abilities. I did not intentionally set out to prove my guidance counselor wrong. I just developed a question that I had to chase. In the process of discovering the answer; I discovered who I really was. The meeting with my guidance counselor striped me of my confidence. I discovered that I must look at myself through the eyes of God. I used the championship mentality to help me develop the "grit" I needed to overcome my educational and personal struggles. Most importantly, I followed God to become successful and his principals to give back to my community.

Journal Notes

MCKINLEY TOOMBS

GOALS

FOLLOW, LISTEN, LEARN, LEAD!

My name is McKinley Toombs. I was born on October 28th, 1969 in Chicago, IL. I was the only child born to this union between Carolyn Toombs and my father McKinley Lomax Jr. I have a sister and two brothers. Karol (Fee Fee), Lavone (Bonnie), and Anthony (Tony). I have two children, who I love dearly. Makina Brown and McKinley Toombs II. Three grandchildren from my daughter and her husband Levi (Tre) and one on the way from my son and his wife Tatiana (Tati). I joined the Navy in 1987 and retired 20 years 27 days later. I've received several awards: Navy commendation, 5 Navy achievement awards, Surface warfare pin, and Master training specialist. I was a Search and Rescue Swimmer, and deployed five times throughout the Mediterranean Sea. I've visited Spain, Italy, France, Greece, Israel, Africa, Dubai, Turkey, and others in the

Persian Gulf. In the Navy I traveled through the Panama Canal four times. I stood on the equator in Ecuador. While serving my country I was blessed to see all these places. There's no way I would have been able to go to all the Virgin Islands. Hell, I was in Cuba when my daughter was born. Continuing that Navy tradition, I now work as an NJROTC Instructor at Proviso East high School in Maywood, Il; where I serve as an Instructor, mentor, and a father figure to 200 cadets. The Navy has taught me so much. I must pass the knowledge on! I'm also a happily married man of two years to my beautiful wife Dana. This woman has literally turned my life around and I am so thankful for her being in my life. I love you babe!

My name is McKinley Albert Toombs, and yes, my first name is McKinley. I was teased a lot growing up for having, as the kids would say, "two last names". But I quickly got over it. My father is named McKinley, and his father was named McKinley, and my son is named McKinley. And by the way my son's wife is pregnant with their first child, a boy. You already know what the name will be.

I was born on the south side of Chicago on October 28th, 1969 and moved to Gary, Indiana when I was 8 years old. It was in 1978, 4th grade; new city, new friends, new life, and pretty much the same environment as Chicago. I learned later that the distance from the south side of Chicago to Gary was only about a twenty-minute drive to Gary. The same criminal activity surrounded us, the pimps, prostitutes, all the drugs. Gangs were everywhere. All the negative things that had become the norm; this was my life, but Gary was cool. It was just like Chicago to me. We were still poor. We still live in an all-black neighborhood. This was my norm.

Chicago was the same as Gary except for one thing… "John will Anderson Boy's Club"! I had never heard of a Boys Club before. Maybe the Boys Scouts, but nothing like this. This was the best place ever! We lived on the corner of 4th avenue and Jefferson St., and the club was on the corner of 5th avenue and Jefferson St. Yes, one block away! Once I went, you could not keep me away. My brother and I stayed at the club. The club was open Monday through Friday 3:30pm -9:00pm. 9:00am- 9:00pm on Saturday, Closed on Sunday. You could say that we lived at the club. It meant everything to me! When I thought that it couldn't get any better, my brother said, "let's go swimming".

The Boy's Club had a nice pool! I could not swim but I still had so much fun. One day I heard that they were offering swim lessons. I had to learn. I was tired of my big brother Tony dunking me and swimming to the other side of the rope where he Knew I wouldn't dare to travel. That was my first goal in life, "Learn to swim"! And once I did, there was no stopping me!

Who knew from such a small thing like learning how to swim would play such a huge role in my life? First, let us stop this stereotype about blacks not knowing how to swim. The club was all black. The swim class was all black. It seemed like everyone knew how to swim or took the lessons to learn. Once I learned, my goal was to be the best! Swimming was an addition. I would stay in the water for hours, long after my fingers would swivel up. In the long run it would pay off.

My brother Tony was a beast when it came to swimming. I remember going to see him compete at the local high schools and just be in awe of him. He made swimming seem so effortless. He would smoke the other swimmers. I admired him so much that it turned to jealousy. He didn't know this, but it's true. He was the best and I wanted to beat him.

Sometimes we need that fire to succeed. That inner voice that pushes you to be great. Tony pushed me. He would take me to swim practice with him and brag to the coaches that I was coming. I was in the 6th grade practicing with high school team. I wasn't ready for the big league, but I held my own. When I got to High School I was ready. All because Tony leaned in.

By my sophomore year I started winning. During my junior year, team captain. By my senior year I was the beast. It was no longer "Little Toombs". It was McKinley Toombs. The newspapers knew my name too. Trophies, ribbons, medals, and multiple MVP's, I thought I was the man. My head was so far in the sky, but my grades quickly brought me back down to reality. I had Tunnel vision. I wasn't looking at the big picture. Now realizing that I'm not going to college, I decided to join the Navy. Some of my best friends had joined: Tyrone Cunningham, Donnielle Haywood, and Dr. Larry White Sr. and others. This was the best decision for me. New life and new goals.

My 2nd year in the Navy, at our morning muster; muster is basically role call and distribution of jobs for the day. Our division officer asked if anyone would like to try out for S.A.R. Since I had no idea what that was, I paid it no mind. Then Someone asked, "What is S.A.R.? The division officer then explained that S.A.R. stood for Search and Rescue Swimmer. My eyes lit up then! I quickly raised my hand and yelled; I'll do it! The Officer laughed. He said, and I quote, "Toombs, you can't swim, anyone else?" I couldn't believe it. They all laughed. This was the first time I had experienced racism. It was so obvious. They thought because I was black, I didn't know how to swim. That's alright, I'll be ok. I mean, what was I thinking?

S.A.R. school was a four-week class down In Jacksonville, Fl. Two white sailors were selected to go instead of me. A week later they both were back. They failed. Later that week that same officer asks again for volunteers and of course I yelled out. This time they allowed me to go reluctantly. It was not a smooth transition at all. I was counseled on not wasting the Navy's money. I was threatened if I failed how much trouble I would be in. They just couldn't believe I knew how to swim. Luckily, I had my high school yearbook in my locker. The section for the swim team had a write up about me wining regionals. That's when they said, ok! This was now my 2nd goal in life. I'm going to become a Search and Rescue Swimmer in the United States Navy and prove them wrong! And that's what I did.

S.A.R. was tough. I was one of the two black students. The other Black swimmer was named Lee. This guy was a good! He was in great shape and the training seemed easy to him. He motivated me to keep going. It was on two different occasions where I wanted to quit, but Lee would not let me. Let's go Toombs, Don't stop, you can do it! Lee kept pushing me. What I didn't realize before going to training was that a S.A.R. swimmer did way more than just swim. We had to P.T. every day, push-ups, pull-ups, sit-ups, and a nice run in formations for miles. After that we had breakfast, classroom, lunch, and then we hit the pool. Lee held me up all the way to the end. I thank him for all his help. We started with 48 students and graduated 22. Lee and I were now United States Navy Search and Rescue Swimmers. Lee leaned in.

My 3rd goal didn't come in focus for years later. Being young in the Navy all I wanted to do was have fun. Making rank was not that important to me. I never took the exam seriously enough to really study. I was satisfied right where I was. Procrastinating was my motto until I met Petty Officer 1st class Roger Griffin. This man was spit and polish! He knew his stuff. He told me to stop playing around and hit those books. He would drill me on Navy knowledge and our job specifics. He was a short man, but he stood tall. I admired him and wanted to follow his steps. Griff was hard on not just me but everyone who worked for him. We did not know at the time that he was only training us to be our best. He trained us well. I started studying and eventually move up the ladder. Griff leaned in!

These are just a few of the great men that "leaned in" to help me along the way. There is plenty more, too many to count. I can go on by telling how Mr. John Cobb got on me and convinced me to go to school and get my degree. Or how my big brother Andre Shelby who took me under his wings onboard the USS Gettysburg and showed me the ropes. And by the way he is an Olympic champion in archery right now. Look him up! When men lean in, we all win! Therefore, I teach now. I am trying to change the direction and mindset of our youth today. This is my goal now. This was the perfect title for this book. I am so glad Dr. White gave me to opportunity to be a part of something so meaningful. It is my turn to lean in now.

Thank you, Dr. White. I love you my brother!

Journal Notes

Charlemagne McCarter

TO SOME, IT WOULD HAVE BEEN
EASIER TO WALK AWAY

Charlemagne McCarter was born in Greenville NC in 1976. A US Army Veteran that is a multifaceted business man and proud father of six children. Spending time with my love ones is Priority for me. Dispelling the stereotype of the black father has been a focal point in my life. Going against social norms and doing my best to ensure my heirs are allowed to flourish in this world despite all obstacles they may face.

This chapter is dedicated to Devonte, Tyrese, Denesha, Charmaine, Craig, and Charlemagne (Malik)

Sitting in class fall of 1992, in a small North Carolina town called Ayden, over the intercom; I was called to the office. My thoughts were running a mile a minute. I wondered what I did wrong. When I got to the office, the secretary handed me a note with a number that I needed to call asap. I called and after the phone rang three times a voice on the other end said, "Your son has arrived." I was full of different emotions from happiness, excitement, depression and needless to say, fear. I was a fifteen-year-old kid, still trying to figure out who I was but was now a father. This same scenario repeated two more times during my high school years. Outside of the school setting, I became a father again during the summer prior to my senior year. That was four children in two years. I constantly asked myself, "What have you done?"I didn't know how to even begin taking care of myself, let alone raising children. My support system was great and they helped financially so that I could finish school. I was also able to remain active in sports and academic clubs and still spend time with my kids.

I graduated June of 1995. It was an accomplishment, but the pressure was great. I now had to figure out my life as a young father of four children ages ranging from two, down to a few months old. I had to take care of them. I picked up a job as a local fast food cook and a few weeks later I started retail at a store in the mall. I was feeling pretty confident but I still felt the need to go to college. Coming from a small town I was determined to leave the area but be close enough to visit my kids. I attended Wake Technical College full-time in Raleigh NC for Industrial Engineering.

Soon after beginning college, I found a security job making seven dollars an hour. My game plan was to go to school, work, and still visit my kids a few times a week. Making money quickly became a priority over school. I discontinued classes and eventually moved to another city for work. I worked long hours and it became harder for me to spend time with my children. In less than a year, I was fired from the job I moved for. I felt the pressure from all angles. I had a child on the way by my future wife and she already had a son that I assumed responsibility for. I was fully aware that these were my responsibilities and I had to do whatever it took to provide for them. I made the choice to enlist in the Army at the age of 22.

November of 1998,I said goodbye to my family and friends and departed to Fort Sill, Oklahoma. Flying and being yelled at without responding was among many firsts.I was training to be a cannon crew member (Field Artillery). Four months after joining, I was called to the headquarters unit of the battalion to receive news that my grandfather had passed away. Devastated, I returned home for his funeral. During basic training, we were allowed three days to spend with family. On the last day, while packing, my son's mother went into labor. I was granted two additional days. While this trip set out in an unfortunate manner, it ultimately ended in the celebration of life.

Three months passed, I completed basic training and remained stationed at Fort Sill. I hadn't seen my children that entire time so I drove to NC. I packed my Ford Taurus with my last son's mother, my four kids in the back and one in the front. We drove 22 hours to Oklahoma. This was a priceless experience because they saw things that they had only previously seen on television. The children also had the chance to be witnesses in my justice of the peace marriage before returning them to NC. My wife, newborn son, and stepson joined me to stay in Oklahoma. For years I would take leave to visit my other children over four-day weekends, leaving Oklahoma Thursdays and returning on Mondays. The drives were tiresome but I was determined to be present in their lives.

I was also persistent in being present. I recall one day while on a field exercise in Yuma Arizona (AZ), I received a Red Cross message that my next to the oldest son had injured himself and requested me to come to NC. To pull this off, I had to fly from

Yuma, AZ to Phoenix to Los Angeles, California to Dallas, Texas and lastly to Lawton, Oklahoma just to get emergency orders done to catch a flight to NC. He pulled through a ruptured spleen and was home before I returned to my stationed base in Oklahoma.

After four more years, I agreed to reenlist if I could be stationed closer to my family. I was so adamant about this that I turned down Hawaii just to go to Fort Bragg, NC. My ultimate dream to be a part of my kids' daily lives was starting to line up. That dream became more of a reality than I anticipated. A year and a half after being stationed in NC, my military career was cut short due to an injury. I once again found myself questioning my next move. I attended school part-time and became full-time dad because my wife traveled a lot for her job. Thankfully my school aid and her salary were enough to sustain the family. In this down time, I was able to spend more time with my children and support them in their sports. Soon after, I began assisting with coaching and reading programs at my youngest child's school. Children began gravitating to me and I took them under my wing. Rides home, fixing food plates, and kids hanging out with my family became the norm.

In 2006, I began a challenging occupation, working with at risk kids with mental illnesses. Two years later, I also began working in the emergency room at the local hospital in stocking. At this time, all of my children except my youngest were in high school. I continued to coach my sons and daughters' teams while scheduling practices in-between my days off. I was exhausted having to coaching the mornings because I worked the night prior.

My life was in full swing but it came to a halt in September of 2009. I woke up in the hospital from being in a coma for 10 days. Although I was grateful to be alive, I remember waking up from the coma and being upset that I missed my oldest son's birthday and my kids' games. I remained in the hospital for a month. The true reason is unknown but it is believed that I had a rare form of pneumonia. I had to learn to feed myself and walk again. After three surgeries I was finally back walking in 2010.

One of the highlights at that time was watching my oldest child walk across the receiving his high school diploma Elizabeth City State University's. The following year, my next son graduated and began his college football career at Wofford College. The year after, both of my daughters graduated from high school. One attended Catawba College and my youngest daughter started a career in the Navy. A few years later my stepson graduated high school in 2015 and attended Pitt Community College. My youngest son completed high schoolin 2017 and now attends East Carolina University. I was a proud father and I too felt accomplished. Despite all the changes and what we endured, all of my children finished high school, no one failed a grade, and they were prepared to be greater by attending college or the military. My greatest sense of achievement as a father was seeing that none of them became teenage parents as I did. Positive and influential presence (Representation) played a major part in this happening along with the support of their mothers and grandparents.

Being a father has and still is rewarding. I'm now a grandfather of six and continue to be present. I extend the same presence and representation in my community. From life experiences and education, I'm a leader in my church's men fellowship ministry. I also merged my military and community experience to start a business using logistical tactics to supplies to federal government agencies with food items and services. Now I also assist others with business development.

If I had to give advice to any father, no matter the age or life circumstance, it would be that life doesn't stop because of choices made or cards dealt. Own it, be present, play the hand the best you can and waste no experience.

Contact information: Charlemagnenow@gmail.com

Journal Notes

_____

_____

_____

_____

_____

_____

_____

_____

_____

_____

_____

_____

_____

_____

_____

_____

_____

_____

_____

Chef Kendall Selby

FOOD IS THE CATALYST TO THE SOUL

Chef Kendall Selby was born and raised in Jersey City, NJ and, as the youngest of his parents' fourteen children; Chef Kendall was often attached to his mother's apron strings. His mother worked fervently in the home to ensure that their large family was well fed and taken care of and she was well known for preparing beans and stews in her massive thirty-quart pots. He vividly remembers watching his mother and older sisters cut up fresh vegetables, herbs and meats while laughing, talking and creating delicious meals and lifelong memories. This was his first introduction to the joy of food and the magic of the kitchen.

Three doors down from the Selby's four-story brownstone stood Big Mama's house; a+ place that bustled with family, friends, music, and a lot of love. Chef Kendall loved and admired Big Mama, and he could not get enough of her mouth-watering fried chicken. He watched as she carefully seasoned the chicken with her special herbs and spices. She would then add flour to the chicken by placing it in a brown paper sack and shaking the bag until each piece was coated perfectly. Next she dropped the chicken piece by piece into steaming hot lard oil to give it that "crunch" that only lard can create. It was in Big Mama's kitchen, amongst all of the sumptuous smells of good soul food cooking including macaroni and cheese, collard greens, corn bread, black eyed peas, peach cobbler and sweet tea, that the Chef discovered his passion for preparing food.

Chef Kendall first learned the art of professional food preparation and catering while working as a sous chef for an up and coming catering business in Northern New Jersey where he quickly grasped the art of turning food into art. He had a talent for recreating meals by simply observing other chefs or looking at a picture. If he saw a dish, he could create it, purely from memory. The Head Chef quickly noticed Chef Kendall's extraordinary talent and entrusted him to prepare the food for high end parties and gatherings with complicated menus using only the freshest ingredients and the best cuts of meat. It was often said that Chef Kendall's food was "too pretty" to eat. The Chef never forgot the chance he was given to grow and excel in the food industry, and he made a commitment to offer the next young chef the same opportunity when he created his own catering empire.

In 2011, Chef Kendall's wife received a job offer in Washington, DC and, with two young children in tow, the family relocated to Waldorf, MD. After working for a prominent restaurant in Washington, DC for a few years, the Chef began to look for employment closer to home. He stumbled upon Middleton Hall on a whim and decided to walk into the building and introduce himself. The moment he walked into Middleton Hall, Chef Kendall felt an instant connection to the building and saw the massive potential that it held. With hard work, long hours and the backing of a phenomenal team, he transformed Middleton Hall into a fine dining establishment capable of hosting elegant banquets, parties and events.

As the Executive Chef for Middleton Hall, Chef Kendall's first commitment was to serve the community. He created Senior Day to provide Seniors in Charles County and the surrounding area with an affordable outing where they can eat, dance and socialize in a fun safe environment. Once a month, Seniors can be found at Middleton Hall line dancing, purchasing jewelry and t-shirts from local vendors and enjoying the infamous Big Mama's fried chicken complete with a full buffet of their favorite soul foods.

The Thanksgiving meal giveaway was spawned by the Chef's dream to feed 1000 people on Thanksgiving Day. In pursuit of this dream, he became a founding member of End Hunger Charles County and in 2019; the organization hosted a well-attended and extremely successful dinner for over two thousand individuals and families on Thanksgiving Day. Chef prepared turkey, stuffing, vegetables and complimented the menu with donations from local food establishments throughout the County.

Chef Kendall also provides a venue for local community organizations, including fraternities and sororities, to meet about issues impacting the community and also raise money to provide scholarships for young scholars and give back to local schools. Under the guidance and direction of Chef Kendall, Middleton Hall has hosted weddings, been transformed into a beautiful banquet hall draped in sorority colors, filled with the sounds of a live band and a dance floor full of people and used to host passionate town hall meetings addressing racial injustice and inequality. Chef Kendall views the Hall as a community center and a meeting place for Charles County residents and he is committed to ensuring that people will always have a place to come together, eat, laugh and fellowship.

When the COVID-19 pandemic came about, the restaurant and food service industries were hit very hard. Chef Kendall quickly pivoted to create an outdoor dining experience and take-out service for his beloved customers and those in need of a good home cooked meal during such trying times. He turned the parking lot and the back door of the kitchen into a drive thru lane where customers could order fresh cooked food. He then expanded into outdoor dining complete with tents, socially distanced tables, live entertainment and an outdoor bar. His determination to carry on in the midst of a pandemic further emphasizes his commitment to continue to serve his community and bring fantastic food and service to the residents of Charles County and the surrounding communities.

Chef Kendall employs high school and college students and provides them with extensive training in food service and preparation. He also teaches them life lessons and skills that will carry them throughout their career. His goal is to groom and create the next "Top Chef" and to pass the baton to the next food superstar. When his high school seniors were deprived of a graduation due COVID-19 concerns, Chef mobilized his team to have a graduation ceremony for the seniors and their families complete with awards and a presentation from the NAACP. He also organized speakers from the NAACP and the Charles County Board of Education to provide uplifting and inspirational messages to the graduates. The graduation ceremony further solidified Chef Kendall's commitment to the young people in his community and his goal to foster a sense of pride and accomplishment in our youth.

In 2020, Chef Kendall created Selby's Food Service and Event Planning. Moving forward he hopes to further expand his catering business with a focus on off-site events and home delivery. The Chef plans to take Selby's Foods into the future of food service and delivery by addressing the challenges presented by the pandemic and creating an establishment prepared to meet the needs of our changing world. He also continues to work with local organizations to plan events to serve the community, albeit at a lower capacity due to health concerns.

Throughout his life, from childhood until now, food has always been the impetus for his existence and a driving force in his life. Chef Kendall believes that food is the one medium that can unite people from all cultures and communities. He will continue to use his talents to foster unity and community service while providing healthy affordable meals to people in need and growing his business to create beautiful events, lasting memories, and the next generation of chefs who will lead and change this world. He has leaned into his purpose and will further his mantra that "food is the catalyst to the soul."

DR. LARRY WHITE SR.

<u>Journal Notes</u>

BYRON T. DEESE

FAITH, FAMILY, AND FORWARD
THINKING

Being the baby boy has its privileges. I am the youngest of four children. My Dad is a country boy from Georgia, and my Mom is a preacher's kid from Florida. We were raised in a working class, predominately Black neighborhood, though it was everything I needed to believe that the American dream was possible, even though we did not have all the things associated with financial success. Faith, family, and forward thinking were the essentials that made us feel like we were worth more than society's value of us.

My grandfather, Bishop Israel Black Sr. was a pastor in the Church of God, a protestant, Pentecostal denomination in the Christian Faith. Throughout his years of ministry, he pastored and served as an overseer for several churches across the State of Florida and help to start ministries from New York to Florida that continue to spread the good news of Jesus Christ to this day! His leadership and spiritual lifestyle were the foundation of how I see the world, and the basis for my daily efforts. To reach those who need to be reached. To create light where darkness is too frequent. This is my foundation, how I was raised, and to this day, how I see that world. Tuskegee University, a place where history was made on so many occasions, it is the only university designated as a national historic site. Tuskegee is the place where a boy who was born into slavery named Booker T. Washington practiced his commitment to teaching industrial education to a society of newly freed slaves who were trying to find their way in a nation who still saw them as three-fifths of a person. Being able to walk past the eternal resting places for Booker T. Washington, George Washington Carver, and a host of other transformational leaders, while I'm my way to class or a chapel service was a repetitious activity that gave me the belief that I was destined to be an agent of positive change, as they were. At Tuskegee, I studied

Finance and Political Science, and practiced it through student activities and organizations like serving as the 1999-2000 National Treasurer for the Future Business Leaders of America-Phi Beta Lambda and running political campaigns for Student Government Association. Tuskegee is the place where I studied in the Washington Library, which details the philosophy, writings, travels, and collective work of Dr. Booker T. Washington. During those years, I learned the true meaning of casting down your bucket where you are, and why Dr. Washington believed that self-reliance needed to become the motivating force for newly freed slaves, and their work could provide a uniting resource to help rebuild the post-civil war south. The spirit of entrepreneurship is the core of industrial education, and after graduating with a degree in Finance, I was more than excited to take all that I'd learned and practiced at Tuskegee, into the world of business and industry.

Monday, October 19, 1987 is a day that I will never forget. While eating dinner, my mom and I were watching Tom Brokaw on NBC Nightly News, as he reported on the unexpected stock market crash, which later became known in America as Black Monday. Tom Brokaw reported on investors jumping from buildings and others who committed suicide due to the massive stock market sell off. I remember asking my mom why we were not upset about the stock market crash? She looked at me and said, "because we don't have any money in the stock market." I was 8 years old on Black Monday, and over the last 30 or more years I have watched the stock markets experience extreme volatility, and trillions of dollars created, providing wealth that will last for generations. This is the work that I have committed myself to since that Monday in 1987, helping families to pursue financial independence and generational wealth.

After Tuskegee, I started my career in Baltimore, Maryland, a city that I instantly fell in love with. Geographically, this city was great for business. A port city that is forty-five minutes from the nation's capital, three hours from the financial capital of the world, beaches to the east, and mountains to the west. In the early 2000s, the Greater Baltimore area had a growing young professional market, and it was a perfect time to form me to be there! In my first job out of college I became a Private Banker for a regional bank, supporting a book of high net worth banking clients. I was focused on learning as much as I could about the financial needs and activities of wealthy people, as I did not know many rich people at that time of my life. I also learned that how much someone earns does not determine their wealth, because unfortunately many of them spent as much money or more than they earned. We would provide loans and personal lines of credit to individuals who in many cases were not in good financial shape, though they may be business owners or directors of larger nonprofits. Their influence would create greater opportunities for the bank, so some of them would become private banking clients because that. I also learned that banking is a very transactional business, which I did not enjoy. I decided it was time delve further into finance and learn more about investments and other financial services.

The follow year, I left the world of banking, and I moved to the City of Brotherly Love. I joined a multi-national financial services provider offering mutual funds, retirement plans, annuities, and insurance contracts. Making the move from banking to financial services was one a of best things that I could have done for my career objectives. I spent my first year learning the basics of income distribution, insurance coverage, retirement plan contributions, and asset allocation. I was also blessed with an opportunity to partner with a community bank there and the local ministerial alliance of churches in low income communities to teach financial literacy in the community. I spent two unforgettable years in Philadelphia, which served as the foundation of my understanding of the financial industry.

Thankfully, this company afforded me the opportunity to interview for a position in England, and within my field of interest. I was a member of the company's sales and distribution development program, and I was more than excited to learn that I had been accepted to join the UK Sales Team! Throughout that year, I was educated on the European financial markets, socioeconomic class demographics, legislative barriers and progresses relative to the markets in the United States. I spent my time working to promote structured investment products to broker dealer firms in the United Kingdom where we already had revenue sharing agreements in America. The people were unbelievable, as I met and spent time with some of the nicest people I have ever met and have maintained lifelong friendships! During my time in England, a good friend of mine named Maria Campbell that I met while working in Baltimore sent me a book titled "The Audacity of Hope", by then Senator Barack Obama. Not only did the book excite me about the possibility of America electing its first African American as President of the United States, but it also made me consider the fact that Maria was more than just a friend.

I left England in the Fall of 2007, travelled back to Philadelphia, and spent a year deciding what was next for me, my career, and personal goals. By this time, it was clear to me that Maria was more than just a friend, and she lived in a city that I already loved, so it was not hard for me to focus on moving back to Baltimore. After reading the Audacity of Hope, I was convinced that I needed to join the Obama Campaign as well, which really needed help in the baby boomer voting demographic, regardless of race. This demographic has been the Clinton base for 30 years, and Obama needed all the help he could get in rallying those voters. After the 2008 election, not only was I excited to return to Baltimore, but I was ready to build a life of Maria, as well as practice my business and political ideas in this city. After returning to Baltimore, and joining a global asset management company, I was convinced that I was in the right city to progress my personal and business life.

In 2010, Maria and I were married and started a life together! The following year my daughter Matyson was born, and we had a family! Growing up, I was blessed to have great men in my life who were able to show me how to be a family man. My parents provided me with a village of loving people, and to this day I thank them for providing me with unselfish love. Maria and I are working to do the same for our daughter, to help give her a strong foundation as well.

<u>Journal Notes</u>

_____

_____

_____

_____

_____

_____

_____

_____

_____

_____

_____

_____

_____

_____

_____

_____

_____

_____

_____

_____

_____

_____

_____

R. Wesley Webb, MBA, MS

POWER OF OPTIMISM

$\mathbf{M}$r. Wesley Webb is the Chief Asset Management Program Manager for the United States Citizenship and Immigration Services (USCIS). In this role he oversees the personal property management program at USCIS offices in the United States and abroad. Mr. Webb's twenty plus year career with the federal government spans numerous federal agencies in the District of Columbia (DC) metropolitan area and Europe. Mr. Webb is an Army veteran who served over five years at the Landstuhl Regional Medical Center in Germany. During this time, Mr. Webb was deployed to Saudi Arabia in support of Operation Desert Shield and Desert Storm. He served his country honorably and was awarded several Medals of Honor including: the Southwest Asia Service Medal, two Bronze Stars, and the Kuwaiti Liberation Medal.

An avid community servant, Mr. Webb enjoys "giving back!" He currently serves as the President of the 100 Black Men of Maryland, Baltimore Chapter. Through his leadership he has stabilized the organization and has positioned the Chapter for growth by increasing the number of financial members and enforcing minimum service hour requirements. Mr. Webb is a member of Phi Beta Sigma Fraternity, Inc. and is affiliated with the Tri-Sigma Graduate Chapter in Montgomery County, MD. He spearheaded the effort to create the Taylor, Morse and Brown (TMB) Foundation and served as its first President. The TMB Foundation is a charitable tax-exempt 501 (c) (3) organization focused on outreach and development in underserved communities. Mr. Webb holds a dual master's degree in Business Administration and Sustain Based Leadership from the University of Maryland University College. He received a Bachelor of Science in Criminal Justice from the University of Maryland University College's European Division located in Heidelberg, Germany.

I am an optimistic. My optimism is a gift that I inherited from my mother and grandfather who demonstrated it daily, even in the face of struggles.

I was brought up in Marion, IN. While our town was not very diverse, it was a pleasant place to grow up. Because my parents wanted to ensure that my brothers and I attended the best schools in the area, we had to endure the trials of being the only Black children in our elementary classrooms; however, the student population became more diverse as we moved up in our grade levels.

As I reflect now upon the school subtleties, the concern for our well-being was typified by grandmother's implicit, though sometimes explicit, disapproval of my parents' choice to move to an area where there were not many Black families. Despite the objections, my mother Lillie stood firm in her belief that everything would be okay. Her decisions proved to be beneficial for my brothers and I, and an early lesson for me in how the power of optimism and a little courage can exponentially change outcomes for better. Lillie exemplified the ideals of optimism and lived it daily. She would tell my brothers and I, "do your best and everything will work out," which was a common theme that was echoed in our household. My mother's emotional strength was linked to her spiritual beliefs. She attended church regularly and I followed a similar path.

In my early years in those classrooms, I struggled with trying to fit in between two converging worlds. My grandfather, Moses Webb Sr., recognized that I was having some problems, so he spent quite a bit of time talking with me. He emphasized the importance of doing my best and letting nature take its course. This eventually evolved into more complex conservations about human nature and the power of common sense; the impact of those discussions further strengthen the foundation for my early thoughts on optimism, even before I truly knew what optimism was.

When I was growing-up I spent a lot of time thinking about things and always had high self-esteem. I genuinely felt that anything I set my mind to I'd be able to accomplish. This perhaps was due to the early seeds of optimism that were planted by my mother and my personal faith.

In 1984, I graduated from Marion High School and was admitted to Vincennes University in the fall of the same year. I remember being so ready to leave Marion because I needed a different level of exposure, and when I arrived at the university things began to change rapidly for me. The most notable change was the unbound freedom, the opportunity to interact with other students like myself in an indiscriminate way, and the values that I started to embrace as my own.

When I pledged the Phi Beta Sigma Fraternity, Incorporated in my second year, I started to form ideas on community service. The fraternity's ideals truly resonated with me, and our motto, "Culture for Service and Service for Humanity," made a big impact on me. As I contrasted my upbringing in Marion with those ideas, I focused on how I could make incremental change in addressing barriers such as, colorism, classism, and discrimination. After all, ultimately, we are all Black. Combined with the foundation laid by Lillie and Moses Sr., these experiences showed me that I was right to be optimistic about life.

When I graduated from Vincennes University in the spring of 1986, I had limited job possibilities, but my optimism prevailed and took me in an unexpected direction. I joined the Army. Basic training at Fort Jackson was a true-life hack; the drill sergeants were merciless from dusk 'til dawn. However, the training provided the mental toughness that I needed to learn how to lead with confidence and to work in coordination with others to get things done.

In the spring of 1987, I completed my basic training and was assigned to the Landstuhl Medical Center in Landstuhl, Germany. I had never been outside the US, and the thought of living overseas was rather exciting. I arrived at Landstuhl and was assigned to the Logistics Division and I was befriended a by Sergeant in the Supply section. He advised me on Army culture and life in Germany; the discussions proved to be invaluable for learning how to adapt to my new surroundings. As I became more familiar with the Germans, I came to realize that they weren't very different from Americans back home.

During that early period in Germany, I realize that at the time I did not truly appreciate the ease with which I transitioned into a new environment. Looking at it now, I know that I unconsciously did not allow myself to focus on anything negative because I always believed I'd be alright. Therefore, having an optimistic mindset gave me the courage and drive to move forward with my life far away from the safe confines of Marion and Lille.

I believe this mindset also made me someone that soldiers in my section felt comfortable confiding in or to help them, work through their personal issues. I have my grandfather to thank for his commonsense advice that enabled me to assist others and always play to my strengths.

I grew personally as I became more exposed to the German culture and the nature of the people. It shaped my perception on intracultural dynamics since the country of Germany is predominantly a mono-racial society and those lessons that I derived from my experiences I would use in forming my own philosophy on building a culture for service.

In 1991, I deployed with the medical team in support of Operation Desert Storm/Shield, in Riyadh Saudi Arabia. I believe that we all have a guardian angel and mine helped me to tap into my inner strength of peace which kept me grounded in a volatile environment. Thankfully, I returned from the Gulf unscathed.

Because I didn't want to test fate again, I decided not to re-enlist and left the Army in 1992. As the saying goes, "when one door closes and another opens," I was offered a job by an officer I served with in the Gulf that would allow me to remain in Germany and to finish my undergraduate studies at the University of Maryland University College. Despite, considerable reservations from my family they supported my decision because I promised to complete my studies. This proved to be a real test for me personally because I had no family and limited contacts in Germany, and failure was not an option. I found myself applying all the life lessons from my upbringing to sustain me emotionally and that fueled my drive to succeed because I was determined to make it.

I completed my undergraduate studies in 1995 and continued to live abroad for several years. During that period, I lived amongst the Germans and became more immersed in their culture and traveled to other European, Balkan, and African countries. The most interesting event that I personally witnessed was seeing the reunification of East-West German and the Berlin Wall coming down. The optimism of the moment lifted the spirts of all Germans and secured a place in world history for their Chancellor Helmut Kohl.

In 2002, I chose to relocate to Washington, DC. It was one of the best decisions I could have made because of the opportunities it offered, level of diversity, educational institutions, and other social amenities. And I met my wife, Mechelle. I was employed roughly for a year with the National Guard Bureau before I took a position at the Pentagon. I was really pleased with how I transition from Germany back to the states and I felt a real since of accomplishment in getting re-acclimated to being back in the US.

Once I got settled, I enrolled into graduate school at University of Maryland University College. While attending the University, I became acquainted with a student who was a member of 100 Black Men of DC ("the 100"), and I began to attend some of their events and eventually became a member. I felt a strong connection to the organization and was excited to be contributing to the stability and personal growth of young black boys. Thoughts from the past about community service were beginning to resurface once again on how I could be an effective advocate for making incremental changes for the better.

Once I finished graduate school in 2007, I changed my membership to the Maryland Chapter of the 100 located in Baltimore, Maryland. In the Maryland 100 I jumped right in again and worked to support the organization on a number of projects to help improve its administration and increase service opportunities. This enabled me to gain the confidence of the president, and I was appointed as the membership chair within the first two years. That appointment set the stage for me to run for the Chapter president, four years later.

I was successful in my campaign because I was young, assertive, and capable of leading the organization. My initial term as president of the Chapter began in July 2014, and thanks to the contributions of my leadership team, I was recently confirmed as president for a third consecutive term. During my time in leading the Chapter, I have successfully launched the following programs and initiatives:

- Saturday Leadership Academy
- Young Entrepreneurs Program
- Virtual Mentoring Program
- Community Prostrate Screenings
- Serving food to cancer patients
- Expanding the 100's programs and services into Montgomery County MD

Serving our community is one of the highest forms of giving back. I have been so fortunate to be entrusted in leading an organization that has been instrumental in giving so much to others and to the next generation of young men. I'm very optimistic about the mission of the 100 Black Men of Maryland and those new members that'll lead the organization in continuing the tradition of community service.

Journal Notes

GERALD A. MOORE SR.

THE RESTORATION OF THE BLACK FAMILY SITS ON THE SHOULDERS OF BLACK MEN

Since black men in America have a long, documented history of being subjugated by dominant members of society, numerous reasons that we could give for our current plight would be valid. Issues which plague the black community —such as the joblessness, the prevalence of gang violence, mass incarceration, drug addiction, and absentee fathers —are inextricably linked to the destruction of the black family, over four hundred years ago. Although some individuals refuse to acknowledge the aftermath of the enslavement of Africans who were forcibly brought to America, the remnants of trauma caused by this unfortunate reality remains relevant today. In 1712, a slave holder named Willie Lynch was said to have delivered a speech on the bank of the James River, located in Virginia. He supposedly informed slave owners that he utilized fear, distrust and envy to control slaves who worked on his plantations in the West

Indies. He outlined methods of indoctrination which would work for at least 300 years, if it was correctly "installed." Some argue about if the speech regarding the best methods to control slaves was fact or fiction, but hardships Africans endured who were stolen from their homeland are undeniable. The dissolution of the stability of the black family is surely a historical truth.

Unfortunately, our collective unit is still in a state of crisis. How many times will we simply listen to the news, or shake our heads in disgust, while walking away when a negative headline about someone brown or black is shown on a television screen? This is the bigger question that I would like to ask you, because I have not yet discovered an answer. I do believe that the survival of the black family in America falls squarely on the shoulders of conscious black men who are willing to roll up their sleeves and put in old-fashioned work to reconstruct black families. During slavery, families were constantly at risk of being divided, if a loved one was sold and forced to go some other place. Today, we must break the chains of a systematic strategy which was intended to keep us in bondage. Black men have a greater legacy than their interruption of greatness. We are adequately equipped to thrive as survivors, even when faced with extreme adversity.

When we consider the bold spirit of men like Nat Turner, an enslaved leader of a slave revolt, it is apparent that progressive black men have fought for freedom, from the beginning of documented oppression. We have survived segregation, and even managed to thrive despite Jim Crow laws and the fight to achieve equality. There are also men in our own communities, and countless unsung heroes who will slip under the radar, if we do not dig for their stories of perseverance. These men and others serve as reminders of why today's black men cannot indulge in victimization and defeatist attitudes, regardless of what outside forces have done. Enough is enough! Taking action to restore the black family is a major key to progress. This is how we can attract better outcomes.

Since we often hear more about turmoil than positivity, it is an appropriate moment to provide current examples of black men who are standing up to answer the call to restore the black family. Knowledge and wisdom can be found in the stories of courageous black men who share their poignant stories in this book. My inclusion of telling my journey to become a community builder who stands with fellow solution-seekers is a momentous occasion in my life. I can tell you about the importance of leaning in, because men who leaned in and pulled me up at critical points in my development helped to change the path of my life. Against the odds, I became an engineer, despite the fact that I once was unconcerned about having a high standard of achievement. I reflect upon my life as a young boy, when I embraced countless stereotypes which should have embarrassed me. Unbeknownst to my parents, I busted out street lights in my neighborhood, broke bottles in the street and busted out windows. Additionally, I did not connect how my rebellious actions depreciated the very area where my parents worked so hard to raise a family, nor did I respect rules as much as I should have at that time. By the age of 15, I was on probation, after getting myself in an unfavorable position with the police. My next step was being required to participate in Rochester, New York's Scared Straight Program. Although I was capable of being a great student, my grades spiraled toward the 'D' average. Then, by my senior year of high school, I became a teenage father.

When it came to making my mark as a football player, I was able to attain athletic stardom. In other areas of my life, I had a long way to go. Looking back, I could have greatly benefited from a stronger sense of identity and purpose, if I had the ability to learn more about the greatness of my ancestors. At the time, there was no connection to the pride that could have evolved from my parent's survival through historic events that unfolded through the civil rights movement, while growing up in Georgia and South Carolina. Since I now respect that era, as I have grown into a mature man, I wish my late parents—Gerald "John Henry" and Carolyn —would have ingrained first hand historical accounts in my mind. On the other hand, I also understand the pain and anguish which accompanied being young adults in that era. I do believe that my parents were trying to shield my sisters and me from unpleasant truths. Although I was unaware of family history which may have inspired greatness at a younger age in my life, I reflect on what I did come to understand about why some young, black males choose to destroy our neighborhoods, sell drugs, and commit senseless acts of violence killing each other on the streets in many major cities. Since I grew up in upstate New York, while participating in and watching toxic behaviors unfold, I am equipped to determine that most young black males have no truly positive rites of passage, when growing from boys into men.

The personal trouble I became involved in could have been even worse, since I was reared in the eighties and nineties, in the heart of the crack epidemic. Boys I grew up with also began to get drunk and high as young as 13 years old, as a rite of passage. Many of their fathers, uncles, or men in their lives presented drugs and alcohol to them, as they began to transition toward manhood. Looking back, it was by the grace of God that I became the man I am today, instead of becoming a product of my environment. Destiny had other plans.

Enrolling in Norfolk State University was one of the best decisions I made in my youth. This place of higher learning afforded me with an opportunity to develop and become a lifelong learner. I recall being able to order pizzas, then studying with my fellow young brothers on campus in the technology building. This positive experience was initially foreign to me, then it became a routine. For the first time in my life, I also was taught by black, male professors who pushed me to be my best. Instead of accepting halfway efforts, while reminding me that I had to be twice as good as white, male counterparts. Graduating from Norfolk State University, then earning a Bachelor of Science Degree in Electronics Engineering Technology, was the impetus which led to a new start. Against the odds, I ultimately took control of my own life and became a cybersecurity engineer, entrepreneur, author of "Motivate Black Boys" How To Prepare for Careers in Science, Technology, Engineering and Math," and the nonprofit founder of Mission Fulfilled 2030.

I now run my organization and an Online Technology School for Black Boys full-time, because I want disadvantaged black boys to experience the rite of passage of success. My goal is to inspire, educate and activate 100,000 of them in the technology field by 2030. Building a community of 10,000 mentors is a part of the process of serving these prospective young leaders. I am also working to activate 1,000 companies who will commit to providing scholarship, apprenticeship, and employment opportunities. I strive to create an incremental ten billion dollar economic impact on the Black community. Thus, my sincere passion to pursue a better future for these boys starts with dismantling examples I recall being exposed to as a young person, while exchanging them for better ones. The rites of passage which are usually passed down to many black boys who are raised in urban cities like where I grew up often involve how much liquor, weed and drugs can be consumed, and sharing stories of bragging rights about how many girls are sexually involved with them. Even worse, doing time in prison is not a shameful event. In many cases, it can be regarded as another milestone.

Despite all of this, all hope is not lost. I can say this while speaking from a place of experience. I had a motivator working in my favor. Unlike many black boys I knew, my late father was present in our home. However, I regard him as beautifully flawed, because his actions often left me confused, when I was a young boy. He told me the way I should go, but his actions, such as indulging in alcohol and drugs, were counterproductive. Dad was not alone. My mother had six brothers, and my father had seven. All of my uncles suffered from alcoholism or substance abuse addiction, at some point in their lives. Although I had other character traits which needed much improvement, I understood at a very young age that if I ever decided to drink alcohol, smoke weed, or do drugs that I would become an addict and ruin my life. Looking back now, I understood that what I observed my family members endure because of addiction, I never wanted to repeat. The data which was right in front of me served as a cautionary tale. The display of their bad habits could have put me at risk of becoming a product of my environment, or repeating any of their choices, but somehow, good fortune was on my side. The good part of my judgment caused me to realize that starting down the road of alcoholism and drug use typically leads to lack of personal control or self-awareness. I witnessed some cases when people who suffered from addiction never recovered from times when they altered the chemical makeup of their brains. The worst case scenario is facing an early death.

One of the reasons that I was able to remain resilient in my convictions was because of a quote my father often shared. "It takes a man to stand alone in the face of adversity. No individual is perfect, but I have the opportunity to be the paragon of excellence for my children to strive," my father said.

Although my father passed away four years ago, I often consider some of his most poignant words and positive actions which have stuck with me over the years. A gift he gave me was his physical presence in my life. Dad was creative, industrious, and taught me the value of having a great work ethic. My father always maintained a job. Upon returning home, he worked in his auto shop in the garage. He was revered in my neighborhood, some of them feared him, which also gave me protection. Ironically, I wanted that type of reverence, so that is the reason why I thought doing negative things would give me respect in our neighborhood.

Despite my father's personal flaws, I knew my father loved me from the heart. Through his physical presence at home, time he spent with me, and his ability to take care of our family, I was able to learn that one of the most critical things black men can do to restore the black family is to take responsibility for the children they helped to create. Although I fathered a child at a young age, I knew that I could not walk away from the responsibilities which accompany fathering a child. When a man walks away from his child, regardless of the circumstances, he immediately lessens that child's sense of self-worth, which can give him or her a lifetime of self-doubt.

The restoration of the black family begins with black men. Damage done to this foundation during enslavement partially led to devaluing us. Now, some educated black women will even state that a man is only needed to produce a baby, but not necessarily help to raise and mold one, since they can rear children to be whole people alone. When theories like these unexpectedly arise, black men still cannot give up on making attempts to be present in the lives of their children. As black men, we sometimes have to face the judicial and court system for the sake of our innocent offspring. Part of leaning in is also facing what is hard, then working to remedy the situation legally or morally, even in times of hardship.

I know a little something about that, too. I began learning to lean in, when I became a 17-year-old father. This turning point in my life ultimately made me stronger, wise, and it motivated me to make better decisions. When I gained sole custody of my son in my teenage years, I faced responsibilities such as dropping my son off at daycare, before I attended school, and also juggling taking care of him while working a part-time job. Evolving into a disciplined father served as a wake-up call that changed the direction of my life, and those who came after me, for the better. Eventually, my eldest son became a student-athlete and scholar who graduated college. Statistics would never have said that my son and I could have beat the odds to become college graduates, but we did!

As a community builder, and leader of men, I know that black men can no longer accept difficult scenarios as valid reasons to give up being the best versions of who we are supposed to be.

The bottom line is that our children need us. The truth is, black women need us to step up, too. As we know, not every child has a father at home. It is true that it does take a village to raise a child. While leaning in, we should not forget to reach back to support children we cross paths with who have no father figures in their lives. Some of us who are in a position to mentor children, but who do not share blood ties with them, have forgotten the communal attitudes which were exhibited by our African ancestors. If more of us offer to lean in, when we see a single parent or child in need, we can make a bigger collective impact. Leaning in entails doing more than just caring about what occurs behind the doors of our individual households. Every human being is equipped with unique gifts and talents. Blood relation is not required to make a positive impact on a child's life. Reaching back to show interest in serving many children whose fathers are absent for whatever reason, in addition to my own, allows me to be a foundational pillar in the community. Our societal value depends upon how we choose to utilize our gifts. Even children need to hear and see that we all have special gifts that should be developed and utilized. When youth are not taught this at home, men who lean in may be the ones who can fill in the gaps one household at a time, one community at a time, and even one parenting relationship at a time.

I have chosen to take my own advice by engaging hundreds of young black males through coaching youth sports, mentoring, and just offering to be a sounding board. The investment in black boys also means that young black girls like my daughters will have hope of having a black men in their lives who will not only be great husbands and fathers to their future children, but these young black males are potential community builders, too. We must have faith in our work, even when we cannot see the immediate fruit of our labor.

My call to action to you is a simple premise. Please do not give up on the possibility of improving life for black boys who will one day become black men. I challenge more black men to lean in as servant leaders, because black boys need to see positive black men leading the way.

I know that I cannot accomplish these goals alone, nor can other black men. Thus, I am calling all black men to make a stand in solidarity to do something to generate more positive momentum, whether it be with my organization which supports black male achievement, or you start your movement. Even volunteering to mentor or tutoring one black boy informally is a step in the right direction. We have to do something civic-minded today, instead of just wishing that the black community was in better shape tomorrow.

And if you're already making a consistent effort to lean in, recruit more like-minded black men in your personal circle to take their rightful places at home and in our communities. If you are a member of a fraternity or professional group, remind other brothers that making a commitment to invest is one way to pay homage to our ancestors who fought for our rights to have better lives. We need to omit excuses and return to the leadership roles our ancestors displayed as a collective unit. Those of us who are conscious, and have a clear understanding of our history and our future, must get involved to promote change. Make a time commitment that works for your schedule. As long as you do something, it is enough! If you would like to join me in a proactive movement that is changing the narrative of the black boys, I welcome you to join me in leading with brotherly love. Please sign up to participate via www.nolongerthevictim.com

Journal Notes

AFTERWORD

The Vision of these incredible Men of Faith is clear in this book, When Men Lean We All Win: Revitalization, Education, Representation, has demonstrated the realities of positive black men making a difference in business, in their homes, and the community. The stories, sharing, and experiences should help you and move you into your greatness. As you digest each chapter, you should have noted and captured valuable information in order for you to reach your full potential using your personal skill set to achieve excellence. As Visionary Author and Publisher of this amazing book and compilation of men, I pray that you will find guidance, understanding, and motivation in your readings.

The depiction and creative intelligence of each contributing author should have provided you with knowledge and skills to further your mindset for advancement in your professional career. Social justice, equity, and tolerance are not just words; they are bench marks for excellence during this time of a Pandemic. As black men especially, we must work together continuously to provide resources and access to information for the youth in urban areas leading up to higher education. During this pandemic, peaceful demonstrations, and the innocent killings and shootings of our young black men and women, we must be remember the ultimate sacrifice has come with a cost, and they way out of the mayhem is exercise to vote in efforts to raise the awareness for social injustice across our Nation.

At the tender age of 51, I have successfully published three books, visited 38 out of 50 states with motivation, empowerment, and inspiration. I thank God for making me an extrovert with the ability to work with various individuals around the world with a common goal of making a difference in life and business.

Just a few things I want to leave our readers with as I close this chapter, as an Entrepreneur, if you only have one client treat them and your business like you are running a fortune 500 corporation. The ability to check all the boxes and not taking any shortcuts as this will serve as valuable working experience for you and future clients. Also, as you become successful, remember how you got started. Stay humble and do things that got you where you are today by attending weekly networking events and community events. Making a difference as a business owner means being transparent and giving to your community. When my relationship with God was not always as close as it is now, I often frayed of circumstances because my faith was weak. But now knowing that the Lord is always there even in the midst of our sorrows, we should always be mindful that is that the Lord is almighty and sovereign. When I am faced with challenges today, I am in constant prayer and the affirmation of my faith keeps me grounding in his grace. In all of the endeavors, I have faced including all of the collaborations with politicians were not always smooth in the beginning. At times, there were disagreements and differences of opinions. In the midst of it all, once I have found glory in doing it Gods way, it became easy for me to make progress with my leadership teams.

An act of faith consists, in its essence, not in religious feelings or thoughts. Religious feelings may accompany our life of faith and religious thoughts may bring us closer to the world of faith but to be able to get to know God just a little bit better. A carpenter gave an experienced fisherman a huge task that was totally against all odds. The carpenter was Jesus and fisherman was Peter. Peter did the unthinkable act of faith which, seen from a purely human point of view and his skill set. He was obedient to the word of the Lord, and did not reply with words, I can't, or this can't happen. It was a conquest of self which exceeded natural limits that Peter achieved. As Entrepreneurs and Community Leaders were must be bold Christians even during the unlikely times but following the word of God until the end.

In addition, as Black men we must support each other more by providing jobs and education in our communities and leading workshops and programs on leadership! Each Author that you have heard from owns their own brand and/or works in a leadership capacity giving back to their communities. Be intentional in being around successful people and learning their habits. It is one thing to have a seat at the table but it's another thing to have a voice at the table.

In conclusion, I pray that this book will elevate you and your families into greatness. I will continue to fight for those who don't have a voice and for those who choose to be still and do nothing. It is our time to carry the torch from our ancestors and hold the younger generation on our shoulders. No more excuses that I was raised without a Father in the home but to do better and not make the same mistakes. Lead your families to victory by being the head of the house-hold and God will take care of the Rest! Amen!

"When Men Lean In We All Must Win"

DR. LARRY WHITE SR.

****

*****

CONTRIBUTING AUTHORS

****

******

DR. WILLIAM D. SCOTT

G. ALFRED PALMER

R. WESLEY WEBB

BYRON T. DEESE

GERALD A. MOORE

CHEF KENDALL SELBY

ONDRAY JAMES

CHARLEMAGHNE MCCARTER

MCKLINEY TOOMBS

BRIAN KEITH BAILEY

DION BANKS

VINCE LEGGETTE

STEVEN LABROI

WAYNE TAYLOR

DR. LARRY WHITE SR

VISIONARY AUTHOR | VIP RADIO/TV HOST | BRAND AMBASSADOR

WHEN MEN LEAN IN
We All Win

REVITALIZATION, EDUCATION, & REPRESENTATION

Made in the USA
Columbia, SC
29 September 2020